Getting a Good House

Tips and Tricks for Evaluating New Construction

by **BOB SYVANEN**

The Globe Pequot Press

CHESTER, CONNECTICUT

Library of Congress Cataloging-in-Publication Data

Syvanen, Bob, 1928-
    Getting a good house : tips and tricks for evaluating new construction/by Bob Syvanen.—1st ed.
      p. cm.
    Includes index.
    ISBN 0-87106-431-6
    1. Dwellings—Inspection. I. Title.
  TH4817.5.S95 1990
  643'.12—dc20   90-42158
                                        CIP

Manufactured in the United States of America
First Edition/Second Printing

Contents

Introduction

I built my first house, with no help, in 1958 in Glen Cove, Long Island, while I was working full-time as a cartographer for Socony Mobil Oil Company in New York City. It was a fairly large contemporary house, 28 feet by 40 feet, two stories, exposed beams on both floors, full basement with attached two-car garage. My housebuilding experience was limited: helping my dad build his first house, lots of reading on the subject, and many visits to check out houses at various stages of construction.

Obviously, I didn't know much about housebuilding thirty-odd years ago, but I had the key ingredient it takes to produce a good product: the desire to do it right. I'm sure I made plenty of mistakes, because I knew just a few tricks of the trade then, but I built a sturdy house that looks as good today as it did the day it was finished.

I've been a professional builder now for thirty-two years, if I use my first house as the starting point. I have, however, worked for other builders in that thirty-two-year period, and it was like going to school, because I learned something from each one. In fact, I still do carpentry work for other builders. And I still learn new stuff.

Since that first house, I have learned a lot from good builders, bad builders, and my own mistakes. I've learned the tricks of the trade, and I know the shortcuts as well. Unfortunately, I'm seeing more of these "quickie" techniques creeping into the building trade and becoming standard.

When one of my sons was seventeen, he did some work on a condo that was under construction near our house. He was amazed to see how poorly it was being put together, for he was used to better building practices. With a little paint the condo looked great, however, and the young carpenters on the job learned that with a few coats of color you can satisfy most customers.

I'd noticed the decline in quality myself, of course, but it wasn't until recently that I realized many of my friends weren't aware that anything was wrong. Even worse, I began to find that those who *were* aware were having a tough time finding capable craftsmen who used what I had always considered standard building practices.

I was further distressed by what I saw on a vacation trip that took me to sixteen states.

—I saw an insulated cathedral ceiling with no eave and ridge ventilation—and an owner who had no idea there was a problem.

—I saw a very expensive post-and-beam house with split trim, exterior trim hard against a masonry walk, and a tremendous draft under the wood floors.

—I saw at a good friend's house a very expensive addition that to me looked like it was the builder's first job after leaving quickie condo work. My friend loved it.

—I also nosed around many construction jobs and saw some really good stuff that pleased me, but that was usually in the super elegant houses. Maybe that's where all the good builders are now, which leaves the middle-income house market (my category of building) short of good builders.

When I returned from vacation, a lawyer friend asked me to check out a house that a client of his had just moved into. This house had been built by a "craftsman," the owner had been assured. At first glance the house looked fine, but as soon as I walked through

Introduction

the front door, I changed my opinion. The trim around the front door was cracked, and the wood threshold at the front door was warped, which diverted water into the house.

The inside also looked good at first, but it didn't take long to spot the huge gaps between the bottom of the baseboard and the flooring. From there on, it was all downhill as far as quality construction in this less-than-a-year-old house was concerned.

There was enough wrong in this house to write a book about, and after a court hearing, the judge agreed. But the whole court confrontation could have been avoided if the owner had known what to look for in a quality house. He could have asked for—and made sure that he got—a house built right.

There are many ways to do any specific job, each with its own end result. The more time and effort spent on a job, the more it costs. But if that time and effort are coupled with skill and pride, the result will be well worth the price. What follows are building practices and techniques that produce the end results that please me, a fussy Virgo.

I'm not the best builder in the northeast, but I am a pretty darn good carpenter. The fact is that there's a real difference between the two. The carpenter is the laborer—the craftsman who actually builds the house—whereas the builder is the person who controls the job. The builder has to juggle the customer, the materials, the labor, the costs, and the subcontractors. This last, scheduling and overseeing the work done by tradesmen not directly in his employ, is the toughest. Normally, this includes excavation, foundation, masonry (entry steps, fireplace, stone walks, etc.), plumbing, electrical, and insulation. It's not easy to make all this fit in with the progress of the house construction and at a reasonable price. To be successful—that is, to make money at housebuilding when one chooses to be both builder and carpenter—is very difficult, especially when the carpenter is concerned about doing the job right.

I mention all this because, in my opinion, it is often this carpenter-builder factor that produces a well-built or a not so well-built middle-income house. (Where money is no problem, it's easy to produce a well-built house: Just hire the best carpenters and take plenty of time to build it right; but even then you have to know what to look for and ask for.) The builder will often cut corners to make the job profitable, while the builder-carpenter will often cut profit to do the job right. As a builder-carpenter, my profit on a job often amounted to less than the wages of some of the hired help. I was happy with that arrangement because the customer was happy, and I was satisfied that I had done my very best.

If you're having your house built, this book, based on my own experience in the trade, can help you insist that it be done right. If you are buying a house, it can help you look it over carefully, critically, and skeptically. You can also use the checklist at the end of this book.

It's getting tougher, but you can get a good house.

GOOD WORKMANSHIP OUTSIDE THE HOUSE
Where to Look and What to Look For

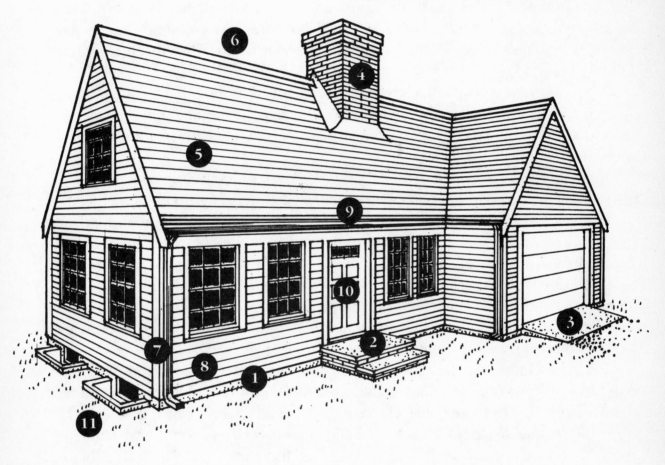

1. MUD SILLS: Well anchored and level.

2. ENTRY STEPS: Level front-to-back and side-to-side. Neat masonry work with no cracks or patches.

3. GARAGE: Smooth, crack-free floor (one or two hairline cracks OK), with dropped apron.

4. CHIMNEY: Neat, clean masonry work with no cracks or patches. Neat, clean flashing with no caulking at the seams.

5. ROOF: Good grade of wood shingles, red cedar best. Joints offset on wood-shingle roof. Good grade of asphalt shingles. Straight line along gable ends and valleys.

6. VENTING: Ridge or gable vents. Eave vents. Well insulated.

7. TRIM: Well painted. Well nailed. No splits. Good joints. Space between masonry and trim.

8. SIDING: Well painted or stained. Well nailed. No splits. Good joints.

9. GUTTERS: If wood, good joints well flashed. Well anchored, sloped toward downspouts. Downspout runoff away from foundation.

10. DOORS: If wood, all six surfaces painted. Weather-stripped jambs. Threshold, if wood, must be well sealed, flat (not cupped) and sloped away from door well. Flashed behind trim and siding.

11. GRADING: Ground slopes away from foundation, basement window wells, ground-level doors.

Foundations

A well-built house starts with a well-built foundation, and this is the way most of the foundations look under the houses I've built on Cape Cod. I say *most* because soil, topography, and the size of the house are the controlling factors in foundation design. My houses are on flat, sandy soil, which creates few problems. For a small house, I sometimes leave out the steel in the footings to save the customer a few dollars in the budget.

My foundation consists of a steel-reinforced keyed footing that has been poured on undisturbed soil. Steel in the footing strengthens it; keying the footing locks the walls to it, preventing them from shifting under a heavy load, and a foundation on undisturbed soil will not settle.

If the excavator digs one corner a little too deep, it's better to make the concrete in that section of the footing deeper, rather than leveling up the trench with fill. This is a good part of the work to keep an eye on. I've caught some foundation men filling low spots to level the bottom of the footing trenches. I've asked them to stop and shovel out all the soil they've shoveled in, down to unexcavated soil, because I don't want uneven settling of the house somewhere down the line. Of course, it's better to explain what you want before the action begins. Very few people take correction kindly, and letting people know that *you* know what you want can help the job progress more smoothly.

I want my foundation walls to be straight, square at the corners, and plumb, with plenty of anchor bolts to attach the house's sill to. A typical footing should have about sixteen 20-foot pieces of steel (commonly called rebars), which cost about $8.00 apiece, totaling about $130.00. Installing the steel takes about thirty minutes. I also place an anchor bolt every 8 feet around the foundation wall, with an additional two anchor bolts at each corner. At $.50 per bolt, this is no place to skimp.

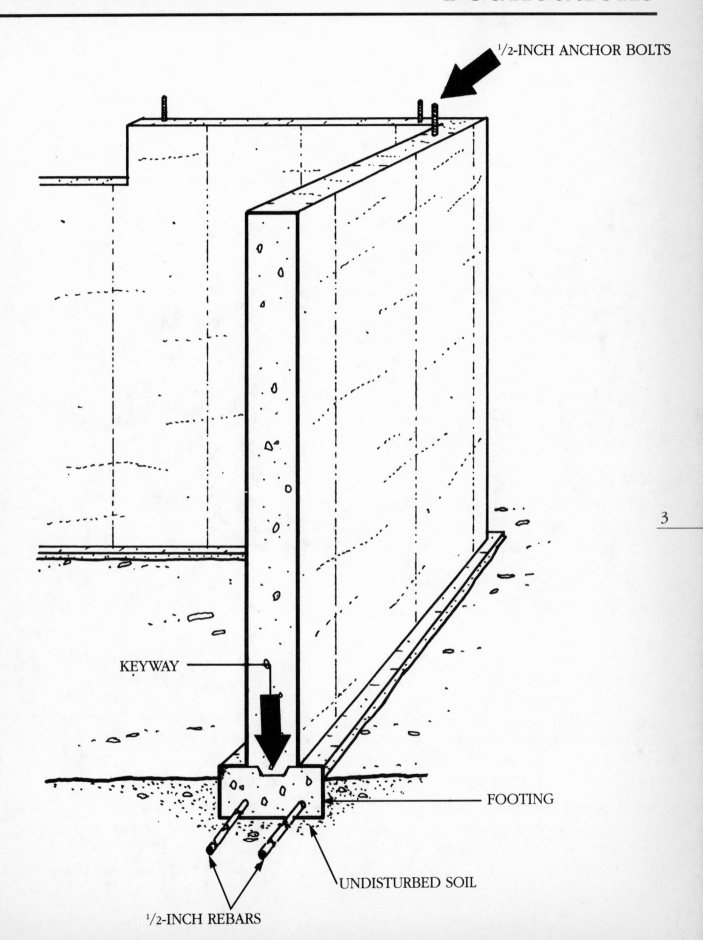

½-INCH ANCHOR BOLTS

KEYWAY

FOOTING

UNDISTURBED SOIL

½-INCH REBARS

3

Foundations

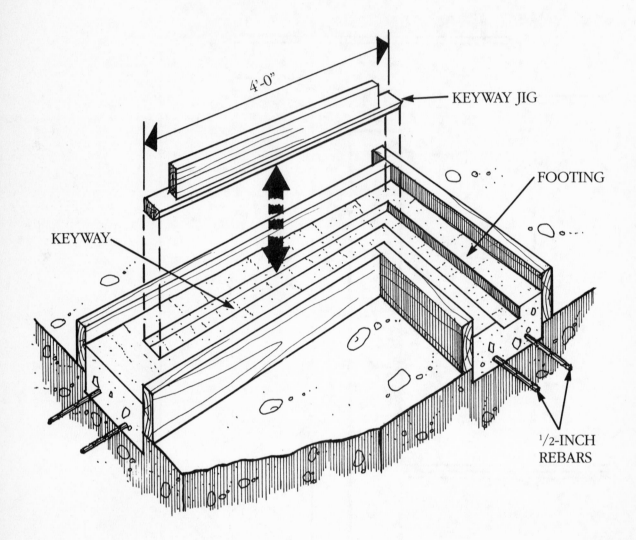

4'-0"

KEYWAY JIG

FOOTING

KEYWAY

1/2-INCH
REBARS

I remember my early days as a carpenter, carefully setting footing forms with a keyway in place as part of those forms. It was a complicated and time-consuming job, but I don't recall a footing that wasn't keyed on a well-built house. Now, though, I rarely see a keyed footing. A concrete contractor showed me this ten-minute method of forming keyways, although he does keyways these days only when he's asked to. Press a 4-foot-long wooden keyway jig into the concrete footing while it's still soft but not soupy. It's not particularly pretty looking when it's finished, but it's inexpensive and it works.

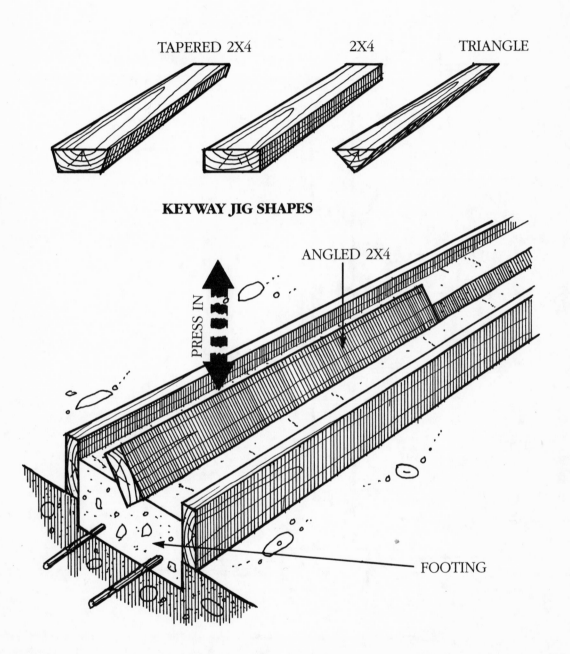

TAPERED 2X4   2X4   TRIANGLE

KEYWAY JIG SHAPES

ANGLED 2X4

PRESS IN

FOOTING

5

I've used this angled 2x4 method mostly because it's easy to press into semi-hard concrete. Pressed in unangled, it makes a 1½-inch-wide flat bottom shape. For house construction the keyway doesn't have to be a complicated job or a thing of beauty. For commercial work the tapered 2x4 is most commonly used. The triangle is often used when the keyway is cast in place, rather than pressed in after the pour.

Foundations

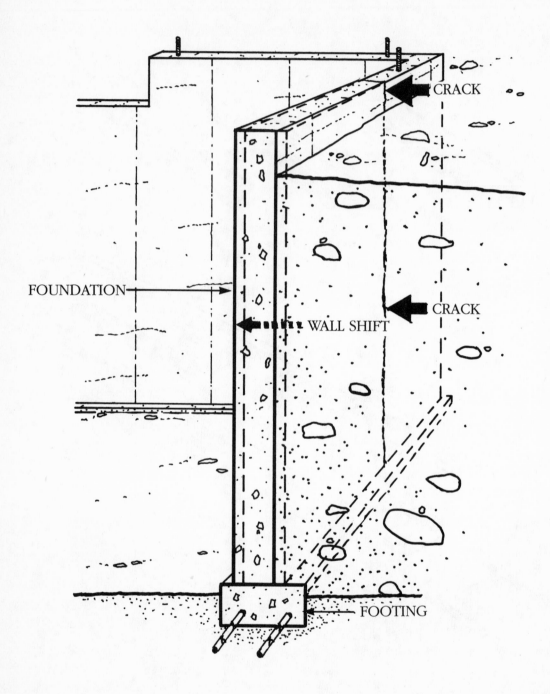

FOUNDATION

CRACK

CRACK

WALL SHIFT

FOOTING

No one wants this to happen—not the foundation contractor, not the builder, and certainly not the owner. Saying what you want before the job starts is always the best and easiest way to see that everyone stays happy. I have occasionally failed to spell out what I wanted, assuming it was common practice to do the job the way I'd always done it. That's usually turned out to be a mistake. Cracks like these indicate carelessness on someone's part, and that is not what you're paying for.

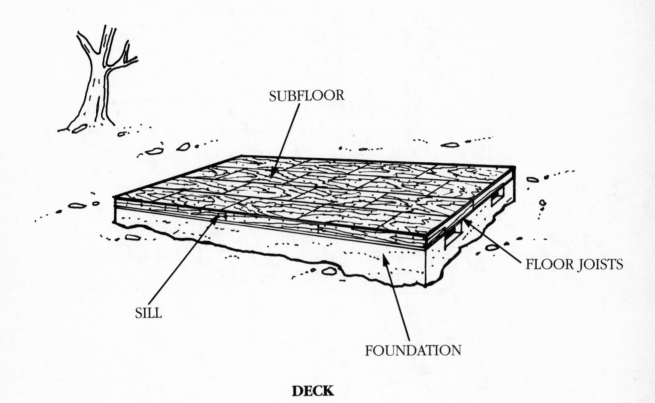

SUBFLOOR

FLOOR JOISTS

SILL

FOUNDATION

DECK

I always build the deck, which consists of sill, floor joists, and subfloor, on the foundation before I have the excavator backfill the foundation hole. With the sill anchored to the foundation and the deck nailed in place over the sill, there's very little chance that the foundation wall will be cracked during backfilling.

Delaying the backfilling while the deck is built also gives the concrete a chance to strengthen a little more. You might have your builder consider the procedure, particularly if any foundation walls are more than 30 feet long. It's easier to put the deck on after backfilling, but it's easier to crack the foundation walls that way, too.

Foundations

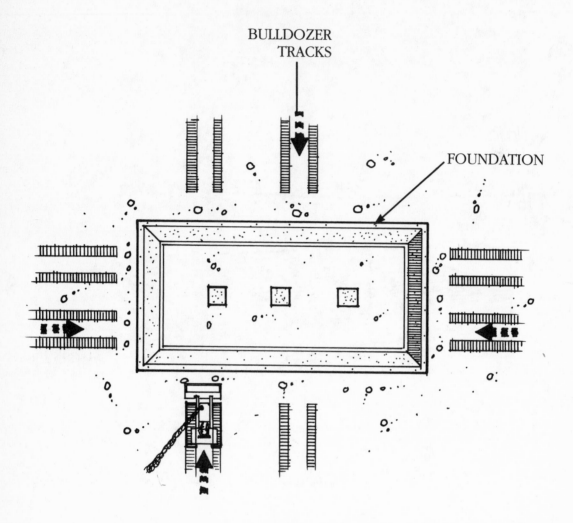

BULLDOZER
TRACKS

FOUNDATION

The best excavator I know always backfills a foundation that does not have the deck in place by working perpendicular to the walls, gently pushing the fill into place. On long walls he keeps checking for signs of bowing. When in doubt, he prefers a partial backfill, because he knows he has to come back for a final grading anyway. Getting an excavator to backfill the way you want him to isn't always easy. Often he will "yes" you to death and then do it his way as soon as you leave the job site. I know. It's happened to me. Sometimes I've had a problem as a result, and sometimes I've been lucky.

BULLDOZER TRACKS

CRACK

BOWED FOUNDATION WALL

BOWED WALL

CRACK

Running the bulldozer parallel to the foundation walls will bow them in. A bulldozer vibrates the ground it rolls over, compacting the soil below, which in turn exerts a lot of sideways pressure against the foundation wall. My first house had wall cracks, but at the time I had no idea why, because there were no cracks in the footing. I now realize that the foundation was backfilled before the deck was on, that the machine was run parallel to the wall, and that the long wall was a vulnerable 40 feet long.

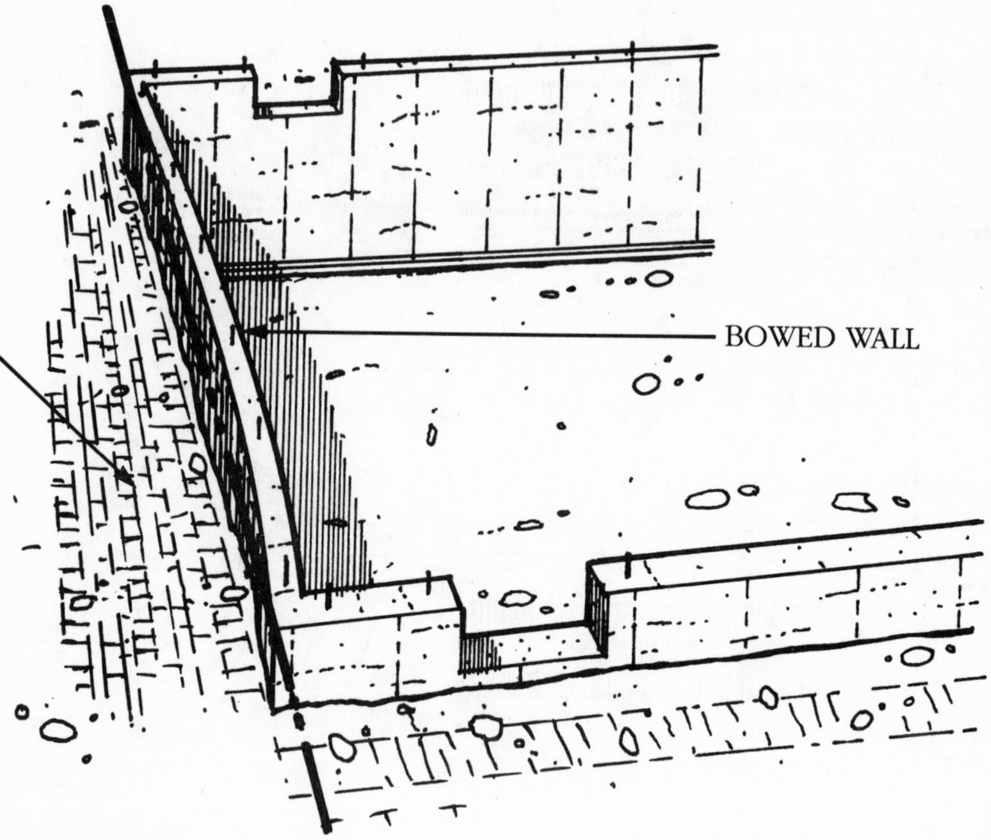

Foundations

BULLDOZER TRACKS

BOWED WALL

A foundation I had done for me a while back had this result: I had instructed the bulldozer operator not to run parallel to the walls and to check frequently for any sign of bowing. He did things his way instead. I was lucky; the wall cracked, but it didn't collapse. It's important to keep an eye on things.

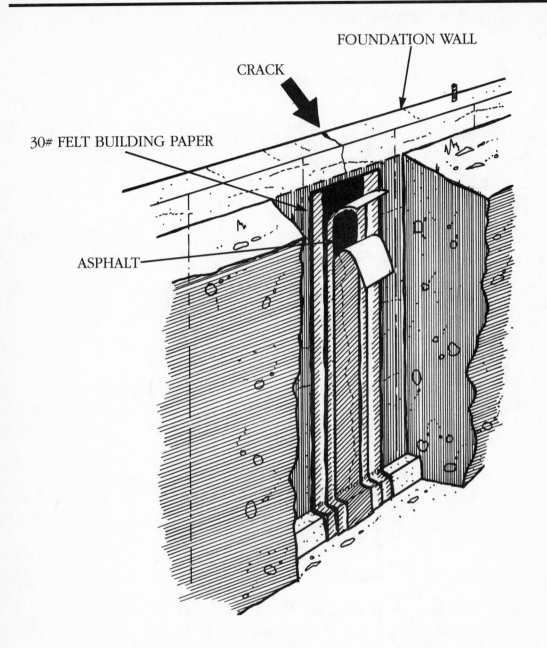

CRACK

FOUNDATION WALL

30# FELT BUILDING PAPER

ASPHALT

All is not lost with a cracked foundation. It can be patched. My first house with its cracked foundation walls was patched with three layers of building paper and asphalt. It hasn't leaked in more than thirty years. There are terrific products available today that let you patch leaky cracks from inside the basement. I have stopped some horrendous leaks using these new products. Nonetheless, it's still best to avoid cracks altogether.

Leveling Sills

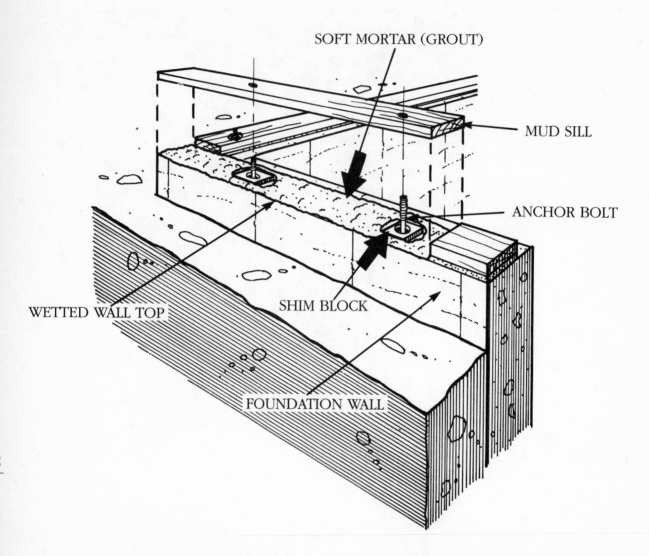

SOFT MORTAR (GROUT)

MUD SILL

ANCHOR BOLT

WETTED WALL TOP

SHIM BLOCK

FOUNDATION WALL

It used to be a common practice in housebuilding to shim the mud sills level and then fill the space between sill and foundation with mortar. I don't see how you can build a square, level house any other way. These days, though, it's common to see builders simply lay a strip of Sill Seal between sill and foundation. Sill Seal, a 6-inch-wide by 1/2-inch-thick strip of soft fiberglasslike material, is a pretty good draft stop, but it also sucks in water and does nothing for leveling the sills.

I *have* seen some current builders shim the sills level with wood shingles, but unfortunately, that's as far as they go. Shimming with wood shingles is great for leveling the sills temporarily, but the weight of the house will compress those shingles; and if one corner of the house is shimmed up and another corner's not, you can picture the results. The house won't fall down if the sills aren't leveled and mortared. If they are, though, it's a sign of good work, and you can be pretty sure that the rest of the house will be built well, too. This technique combines shimming and grouting in one step. It's quicker but more difficult than the following technique.

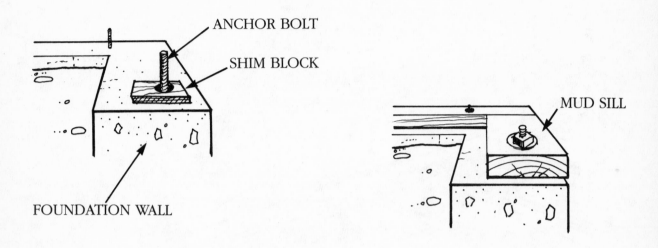

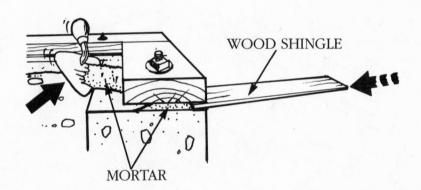

This technique, similar to the standard old-fashioned approach, is a good, quick way to get the mud sills in place, followed by the deck, before packing the grout in. You can come back, shim the sill up against the floor framing, and grout any time. It allows the rest of the job to progress, but grouting this way is a slow process.

The steps are as follows:

1. Install leveling shim blocks at each anchor bolt.

2. Bolt mud sills in place.

3. Shim mud sills up against floor framing.

4. Grout anytime by throwing mortar into the space between the mud sill and the top of the foundation wall. Pack it in with the butt (thick) end of a wood shingle.

On a house I did a few years ago I used both methods, and I was surprised at how long it took my $15.00-an-hour man to pack mortar under the sills. I'm sure the main reason sill grouting isn't done today is this cost of labor. That's why I came up with the faster technique shown on the previous page.

Gluing Subfloors

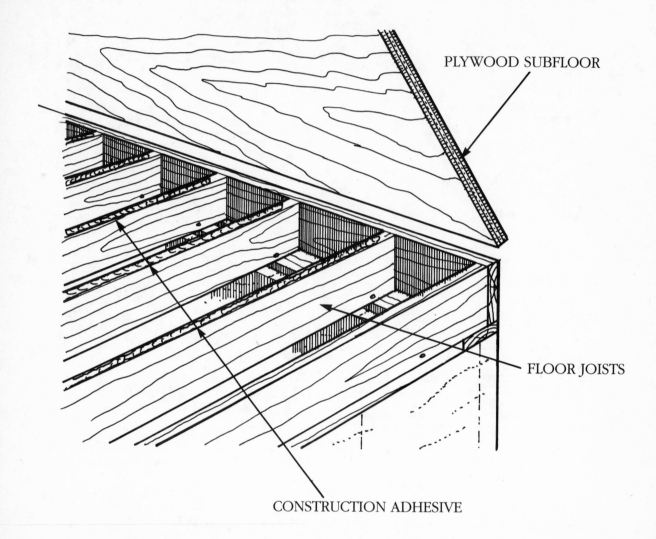

PLYWOOD SUBFLOOR

FLOOR JOISTS

CONSTRUCTION ADHESIVE

I mentioned earlier that it's best to put the deck on before backfilling the foundation. Well, if you glue the subfloor in place using a construction adhesive (PL 200 or PL 400), you'll go a long way toward preventing squeaky floors. A bed of adhesive on top of each floor joist, along with the standard nailing, eliminates the movement that produces squeaks. (There's no need to waste adhesive on the perimeter framing members because the exterior walls will hold them in place.)

This is another one of those things you have to ask your builder to do. In a house that's already built, you can check in the basement to see if you can spot adhesive oozing out along the top of the floor joists. Gluing is a relatively new technique, so it doesn't mean bad work if it wasn't done. In fact, I started doing it only about five years ago.

Masonry Entrance Steps

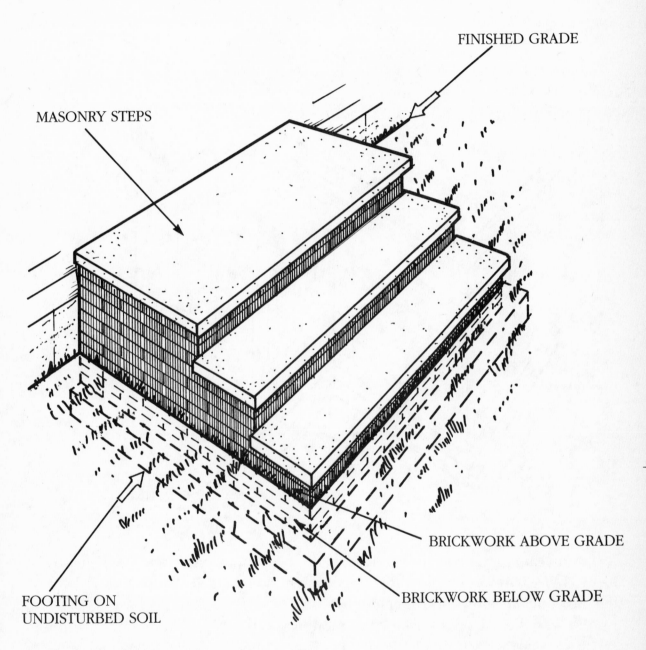

FINISHED GRADE

MASONRY STEPS

BRICKWORK ABOVE GRADE

BRICKWORK BELOW GRADE

FOOTING ON
UNDISTURBED SOIL

Masonry steps are extremely heavy and they require a good strong footing on undisturbed soil to prevent sags and cracks. Unfortunately, the soil at the entry area is always soft fill, not suitable for supporting heavy loads such as masonry steps. I've had to repair quite a few entry steps built on slabs that have been poured on this stuff.

Masonry Entrance Steps

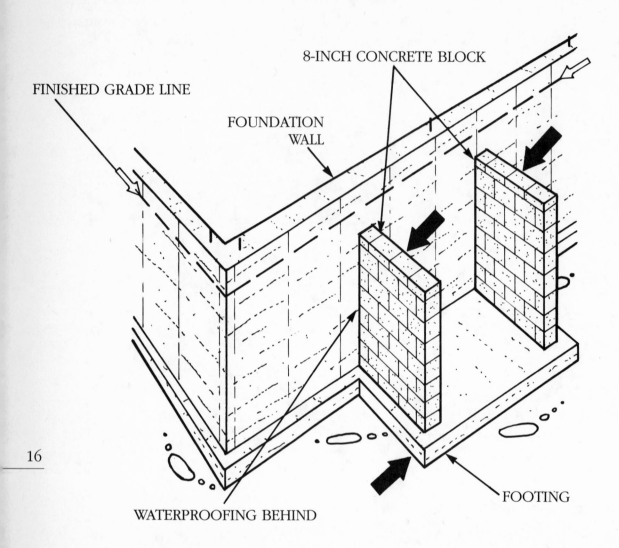

8-INCH CONCRETE BLOCK

FINISHED GRADE LINE

FOUNDATION WALL

WATERPROOFING BEHIND

FOOTING

A dozen years ago, a mason friend showed me a simple, easy, and inexpensive method that I always use now for supporting masonry steps. A nice feature here is that no concrete shows above grade.

For very heavy loads I use two or more walls of 8-inch concrete block supported by a footing, which should be poured as part of the foundation-wall footing. The concrete blocks are laid up dry, without mortar. The top of the block walls should be well below the finished grade. The top of the reinforced concrete slab supported by the block walls will then be below grade, so that only the finished material—brick or stone—will show above grade. For lighter-weight steps I've laid the blocks on undisturbed soil with no concrete footing.

A nice side benefit to this method is that the waterproofing that is brushed onto the outside of the foundation wall becomes an unbroken membrane behind the concrete-block walls because the blocks are laid up after the waterproofing is applied.

Masonry Entrance Steps

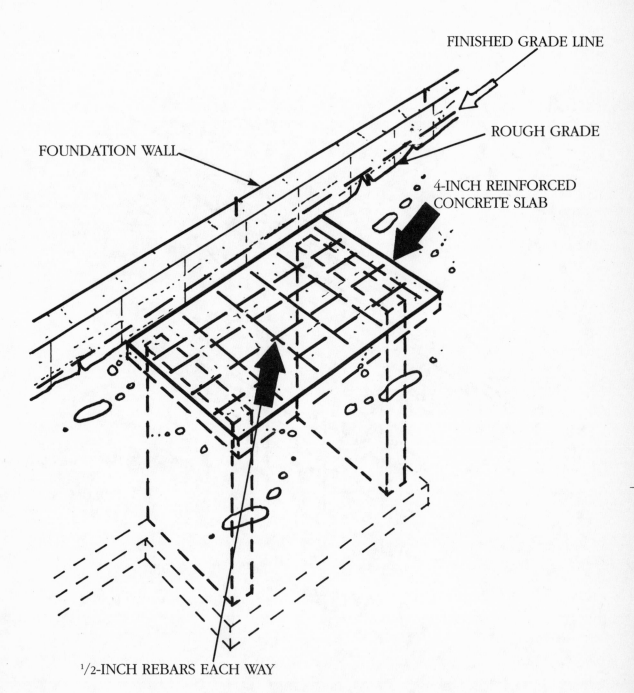

FINISHED GRADE LINE

ROUGH GRADE

FOUNDATION WALL

4-INCH REINFORCED CONCRETE SLAB

¹/₂-INCH REBARS EACH WAY

The concrete-block walls support a 4-inch concrete slab with ¹/₂-inch rebars running each way, with about a 12-inch grid. None of this work is very time consuming or precise. The concrete slab should be level and large enough to accommodate the finished masonry steps. There are other ways to support masonry steps, but this method works well for me. It allows freedom to change the step design. Once again, you will have to show your builder what you want, but if he or she is a good builder, the merits of this method will be obvious.

Masonry Entrance Steps

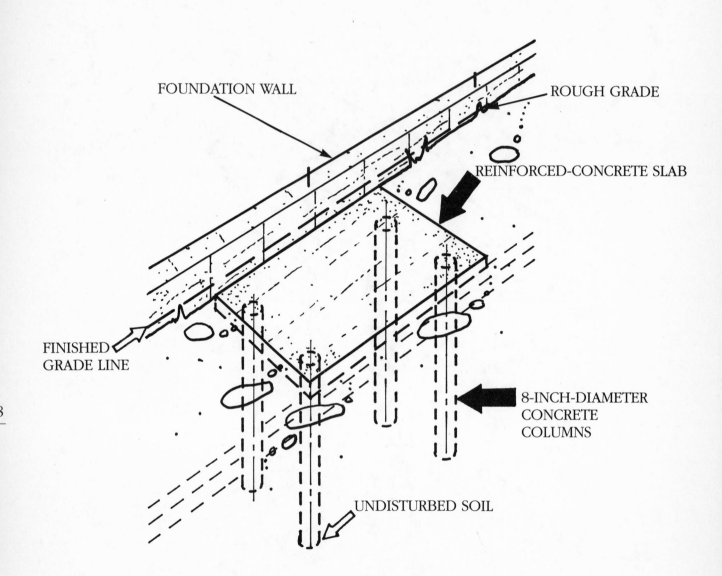

FOUNDATION WALL

ROUGH GRADE

REINFORCED-CONCRETE SLAB

FINISHED GRADE LINE

8-INCH-DIAMETER CONCRETE COLUMNS

UNDISTURBED SOIL

Supporting the reinforced slab-on-concrete posts is a system to use when no footing or support walls are in place. Compared with scooping out a 7-foot pit, digging four 7-foot holes with a post-hole digger is relatively easy work. I've done this for small masonry steps and when a remodel job called for a new entry.

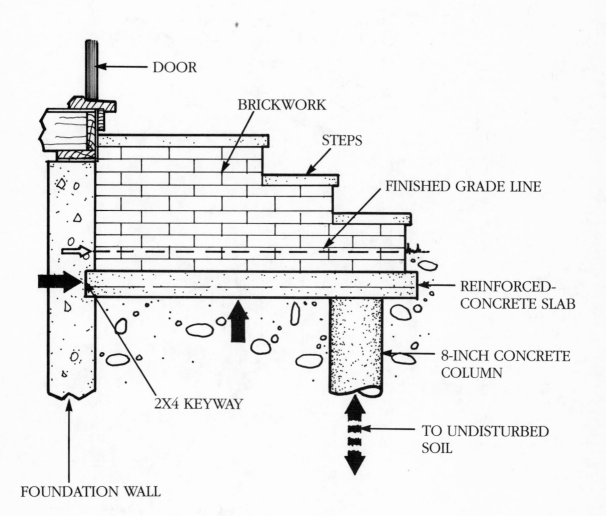

DOOR

BRICKWORK

STEPS

FINISHED GRADE LINE

REINFORCED-
CONCRETE SLAB

8-INCH CONCRETE
COLUMN

TO UNDISTURBED
SOIL

2X4 KEYWAY

FOUNDATION WALL

19

This is another variation, which works best when the finished grade is known. A 2x4 keyway in the foundation wall supports the reinforced-concrete slab at the foundation end. Eight-inch concrete columns support the slab at the outer edge. The problem with this system is its lack of flexibility. The keyway must be below grade, so once the keyway is located, the grade can't be lowered below the top of the key-way without exposing the unattractive reinforced slab.

Garage Floors and Aprons

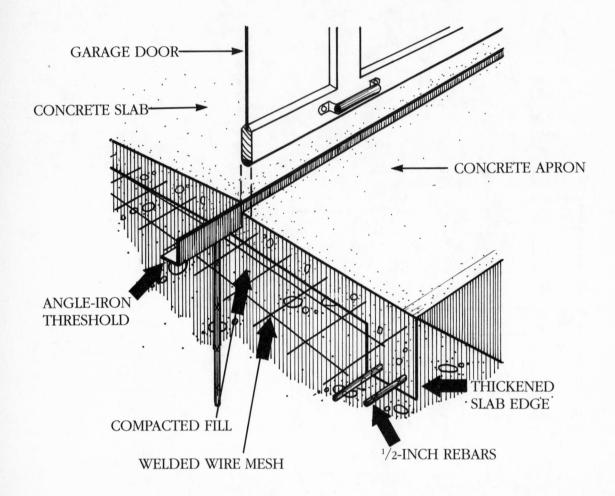

GARAGE DOOR

CONCRETE SLAB

CONCRETE APRON

ANGLE-IRON
THRESHOLD

COMPACTED FILL

WELDED WIRE MESH

1/2-INCH REBARS

THICKENED
SLAB EDGE

A good garage floor has a smooth, crack-free concrete slab and an apron that is sloped slightly to drain water out and away from the garage. The concrete apron, which is outside the garage, should be ³/₄ inch lower than the concrete slab inside the garage. The closed garage door should rest on the lower concrete apron. This keeps wind-driven leaves and water out of the garage.

The way I get a good long-lasting garage floor and apron is to make sure the concrete is poured on *well-compacted* fill. I like sand best. Both the slab and the apron should be reinforced with welded wire mesh embedded in them. I thicken the driveway edge of the apron and put in two steel rebars. I reinforce the garage-floor slab at the dropped apron with a continuous piece of angle iron. These are features you have to ask for specifically because garages are not generally done this way, and there's no way of knowing, other than by the angle iron, if it has been done.

Garage Floors and Aprons

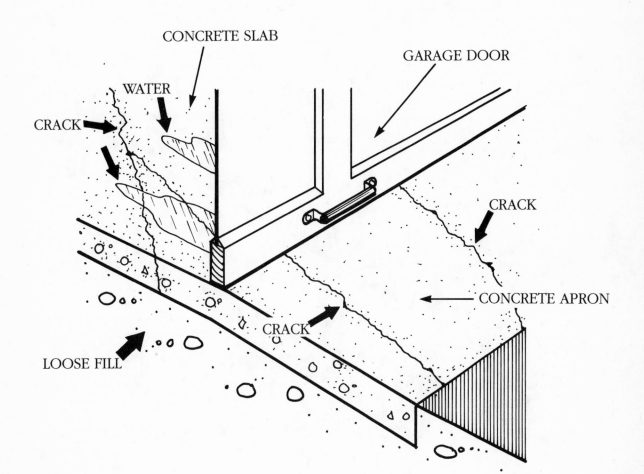

CONCRETE SLAB

GARAGE DOOR

WATER

CRACK

CRACK

CONCRETE APRON

CRACK

LOOSE FILL

Here is what you often see: a cracked apron, cracked slabs, and water leaks under doors. Thin concrete slabs on soft fill won't hold up under the stress of everyday car traffic. Without a dropped apron, it's difficult to keep water and dirt out of the garage. Even a simple dropped apron with no angle iron will work, but it's easier to get a flat level floor when a length of angle iron is used. Properly set in place, it acts as a form to contain the concrete when it's poured and screeded.

Garage Floors and Aprons

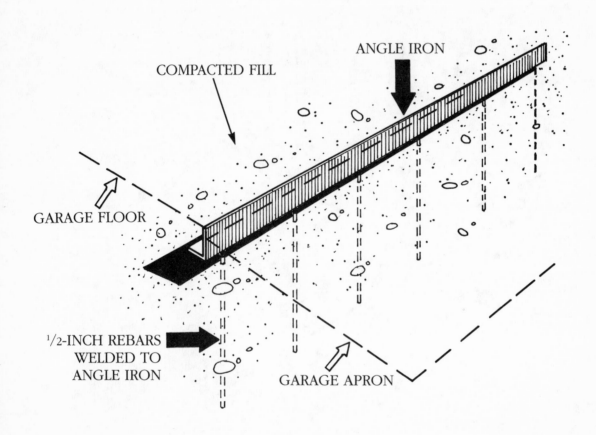

COMPACTED FILL

ANGLE IRON

GARAGE FLOOR

¹/2-INCH REBARS
WELDED TO
ANGLE IRON

GARAGE APRON

It's neither difficult nor expensive to install an angle-iron strip at the garage-door opening. A few lengths of rebar welded to angle iron (which any welding shop can do) serve to support it in place during the concrete pour. The angle iron is simply located an inch or so behind where the back of the door will be and then driven down with a hand maul to the height desired to make sure it's level. This is a quick, inexpensive, dynamite system for creating a dropped apron and reinforcing the slab at the garage door.

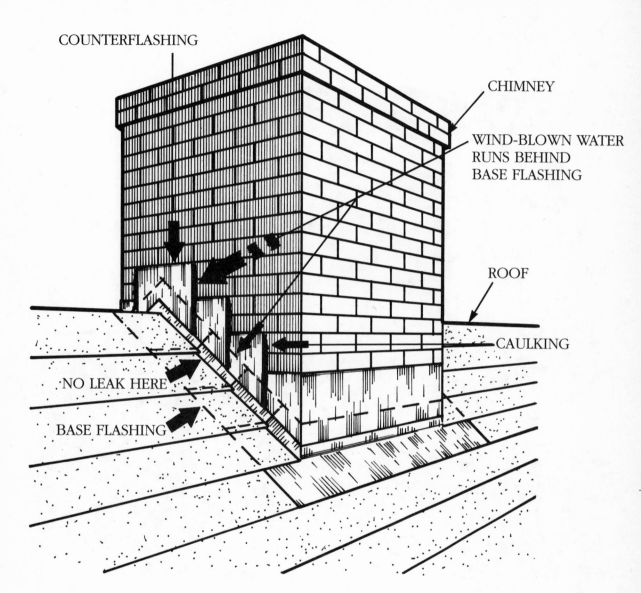

COUNTERFLASHING

CHIMNEY

WIND-BLOWN WATER RUNS BEHIND BASE FLASHING

ROOF

CAULKING

NO LEAK HERE

BASE FLASHING

The next time you're driving or walking around your neighborhood, take a look at the chimneys of the older houses and you'll see another all-too-common sight: caulked chimney flashing. The caulking is an effort to stop wind-driven water from getting into the house and staining the ceiling and walls below. Aside from looking bad, the caulking is always only temporary because there is so much expansion and contraction of the different materials that the cracks don't stay closed. You won't see caulking on new chimneys because it takes a few years for things to happen. Not all chimneys have this problem, but I have patched and repatched an awful lot of chimney flashing on Cape Cod, where I live.

Chimneys

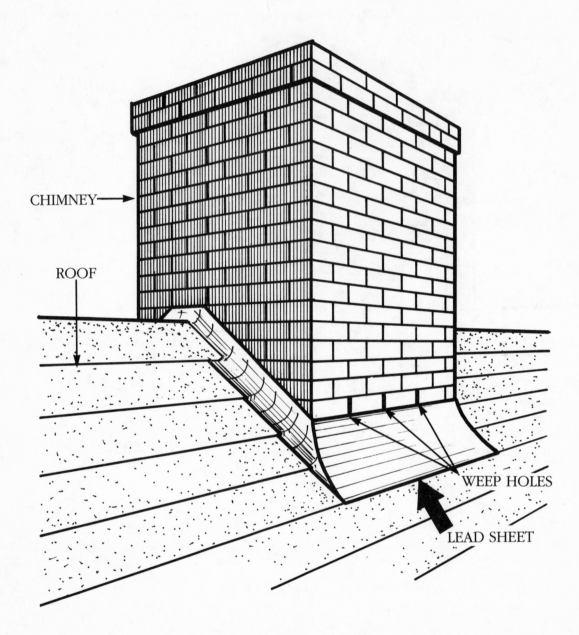

CHIMNEY

ROOF

WEEP HOLES

LEAD SHEET

This chimney flashing system, called a through lead pan flashing, will not leak. It costs $200 to $300 more than conventional chimney flashing, but you'll never have to worry about leaking. I've seen this flashing system used only on Cape Cod, but it's been used successfully here for more than 50 years. It takes know-how and skill to flash a chimney using this system, and many masons have never heard of it, so you might have difficulty finding a mason to use it.

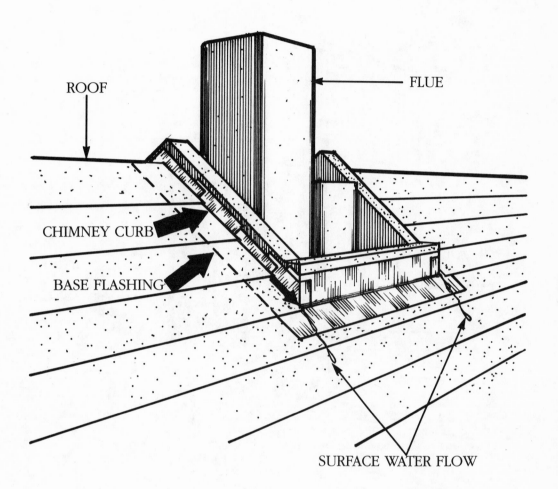

ROOF

FLUE

CHIMNEY CURB

BASE FLASHING

SURFACE WATER FLOW

The chimney is base-flashed (horizontally under the shingle courses, and vertically against the chimney base) normally. This keeps water running down the roof from getting into the house below. My mason convinced me to use the through lead pan flashing system when he told me about the fifty-year-old lead pan–flashed chimney he was asked to check out because it leaked. He spent hours on the roof, running water from a garden hose from every possible direction and checking the flashing for tears. He suddenly realized that the roof had just been reshingled and that the leak was a new one. The light went on! The roofers had improperly replaced a piece of base flashing, and it was diverting water into the house instead of onto the roof. A five-minute fix was all it took, and no more leak. The fifty-year-old through lead pan flashing had not failed after all.

Chimneys

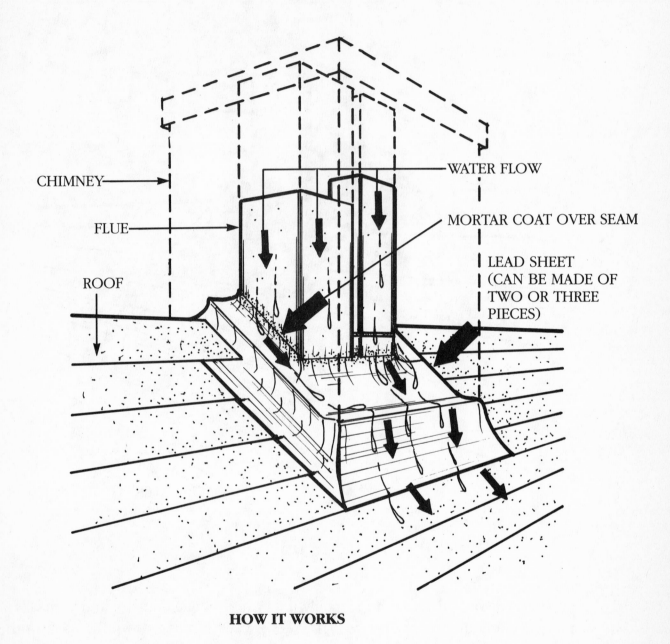

CHIMNEY

FLUE

ROOF

WATER FLOW

MORTAR COAT OVER SEAM

LEAD SHEET
(CAN BE MADE OF
TWO OR THREE
PIECES)

HOW IT WORKS

The secret to the success of this flashing is the lead sheeting. Internally, the lead is shaped to divert any water that gets behind the chimney brickwork away from the flues. All the internal water, and there is plenty of it, is diverted out the weep holes and onto the roof. The base flashing is completely covered by the lead sheeting, resulting in a nonleaking chimney flashing system. When the roof must be replaced, the lead sheet that was folded down onto the roof is merely lifted for the removal of the old shingles underneath. The sheet is then patted back down after the new shingles are on the roof.

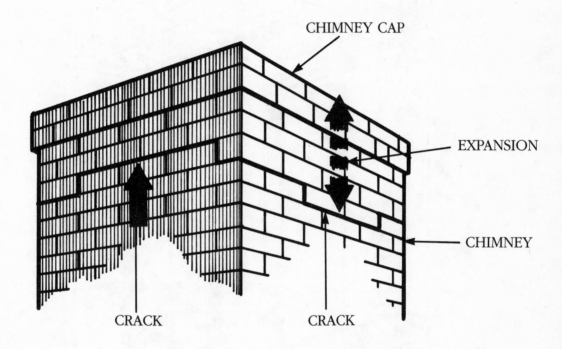

CHIMNEY CAP

EXPANSION

CHIMNEY

CRACK   CRACK

Another common problem is chimney cracks. The top of a chimney usually has a sloped concrete cap cast in place around the chimney flues. When the flues expand from fireplace or furnace heat, they will lift the cap and all attached masonry. The results are cracks at the weakest parts of the masonry chimney. When the chimney comes through the roof, the cracks are usually around its top. When the chimney is on the outside wall, the cracks can be wherever the masonry is weakest. These cracks aren't a structural problem, but they look awful.

Chimneys

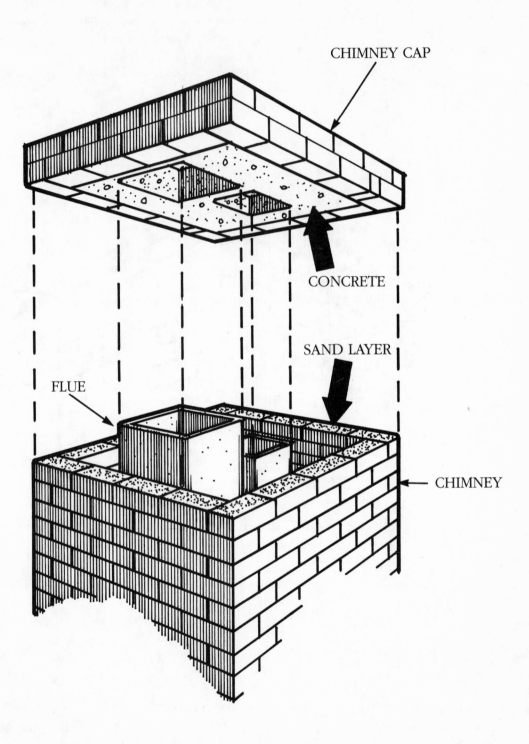

CHIMNEY CAP

CONCRETE

SAND LAYER

FLUE

CHIMNEY

The way to overcome this problem is to force the masonry to crack where you want it to: in other words, to make a control joint, usually by sprinkling sand under a mortar joint. An overhang brick course is a good place for such a control joint. The resulting crack in the shadow will be virtually invisible. Your mason should be able to figure out how to do this if he knows his craft.

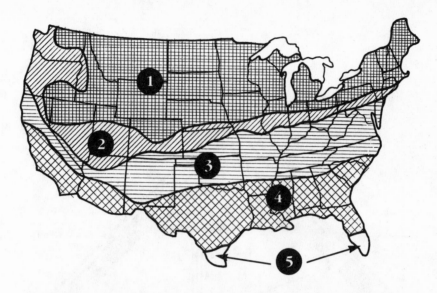

RECOMMENDED INSULATION R-VALUES BY REGION

Zones	Ceiling R-Value	Wall R-Value	Floor R-Value
1	R-49	R-19	R-25
2	R-38	R-19	R-19
3	R-38	R-19	R-13
4	R-30	R-19	R-11
5	R-19	R-12	R-11

Insulation is rated by "R" value. It's not important to know what that is, but it is important to know that the R-value per inch of fiberglass insulation ranges from 2.5-R to 3.6-R, depending on its density. If you figure on R-3 per inch, you'll be pretty close.

In a tight house the difference in temperature between floor and ceiling is around three to five degrees. It can be as high as fifteen degrees in a house with uninsulated floors and leaky doors and windows. So to maintain a comfortable temperature in a house, it's important to reduce infiltration and exfiltration.

Infiltration can be reduced by installing good weatherstripped windows and exterior doors. The best exterior door unit I've found is metal. Metal doors are insulated, they're weatherstripped almost like a refrigerator, and they won't warp.

Exfiltration can be reduced by careful ceiling installation. There should be no gaps in the insulation, and it should be cut to fit snugly around framing members and any pipes leading into the attic. Insist on having it done that way, and then check to make sure it was done right. I've called back a few insulation contractors because of faulty work, and they have always made things right.

Fiberglass isn't the only insulating material available, and some alternatives have specialized applications. Rigid foam panels are used for insulating foundation walls and cathedral ceilings. They are used in conjunction with fiberglass to increase R-values. These panels are more expensive per R-value than fiberglass, and ants love the stuff, so beware! Rockwool and cellulose are used mostly for blown-in applications.

Insulation

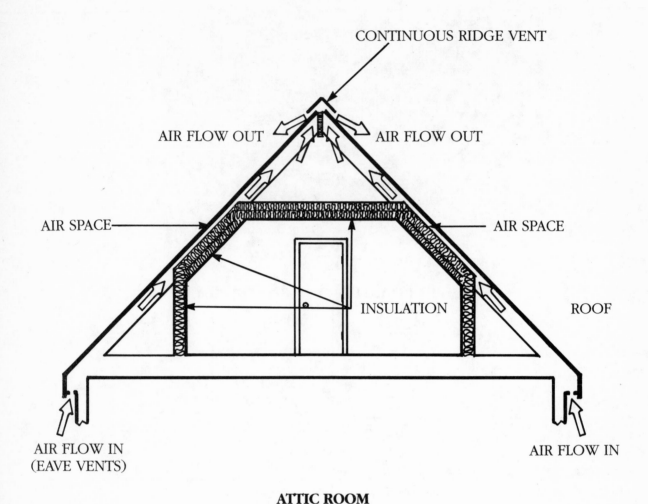

CONTINUOUS RIDGE VENT

AIR FLOW OUT — AIR FLOW OUT

AIR SPACE — AIR SPACE

INSULATION — ROOF

AIR FLOW IN
(EAVE VENTS) — AIR FLOW IN

ATTIC ROOM

In cold climates, moisture driven from the warm interior of a house through insulation often condenses on cold sheathing surfaces and then drips back onto the insulation, reducing the insulation's effectiveness. In warm humid climates, hot outside air can condense on cooled sheathing or framing members.

A properly placed vapor barrier will prevent *most* of the water vapor from reaching the cool surfaces. It should be placed on the *interior* side of the wall in a heating situation, and on the *outside* of a wall in a cooling situation. Where to put the vapor barrier in a house that is both heated and cooled remains unsolved.

Ventilation is the way to get rid of any water vapor that does get through. The rule of thumb is that attics need 1 square foot of venting for every 150 square feet of ceiling in the rooms below. Attics with a vapor barrier in the ceilings below need 1 square foot of venting for every 300 square feet of ceiling. After a house is built, you usually can't tell if there is a vapor barrier and a ventilating air space or not, but any staining of the wall or sloped ceiling is a sign that air space and vapor barrier are not there.

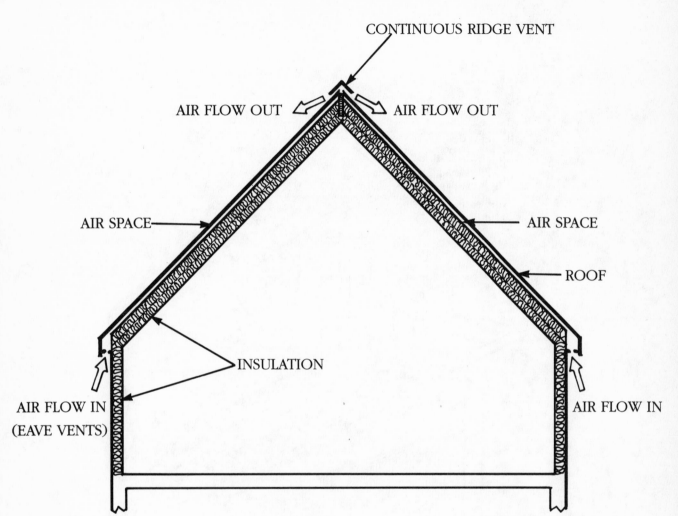

CATHEDRAL CEILING

The natural flow of air is to rise as it heats. Screened vents at the eaves allow air to rise along the air space and exit through a continuous roof vent.

The cathedral ceiling is not as common as the attic room, but the same precautions must be taken to prevent condensation problems from occurring. There must be a free flow of air from the eaves to the ridge vents with no blocked or dead areas. Watch for blocked or dead areas at skylights and chimneys. Your builder must drill holes through the top of the rafters (where they are blocked off by a skylight or chimney) to allow free passage of air from the dead-end rafter space into the next free-rafter space that runs to the ridge.

Without proper venting and vapor barriers, your ceilings will become stained black by the retained condensed water, and both your roof sheathing and rafters will rot. My daughter and son-in-law live in such a house, and while there is no rot yet, the wood ceiling shows the telltale black stains.

Insulation

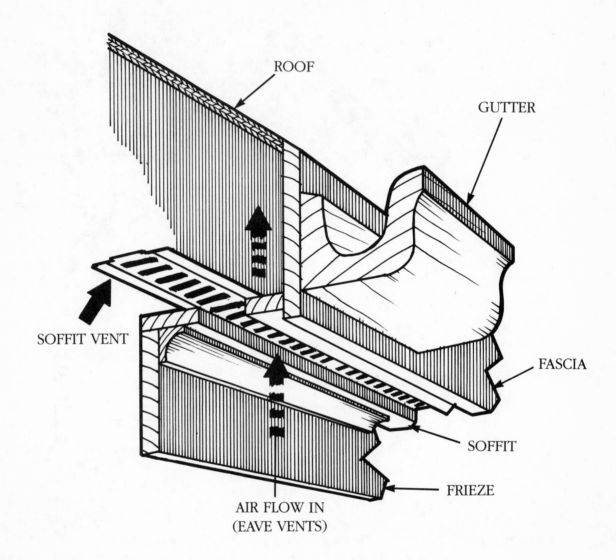

ROOF

GUTTER

SOFFIT VENT

FASCIA

SOFFIT

FRIEZE

AIR FLOW IN
(EAVE VENTS)

Continuous screened eave venting is easy to install and inexpensive. It's available at most lumberyards. These aluminum strips blend into any trim style.

If you see no vents, the house is not properly vented. It's as simple as that. All is not lost, however, because small, round vents, called Midget Louvers, can be easily installed into drilled holes.

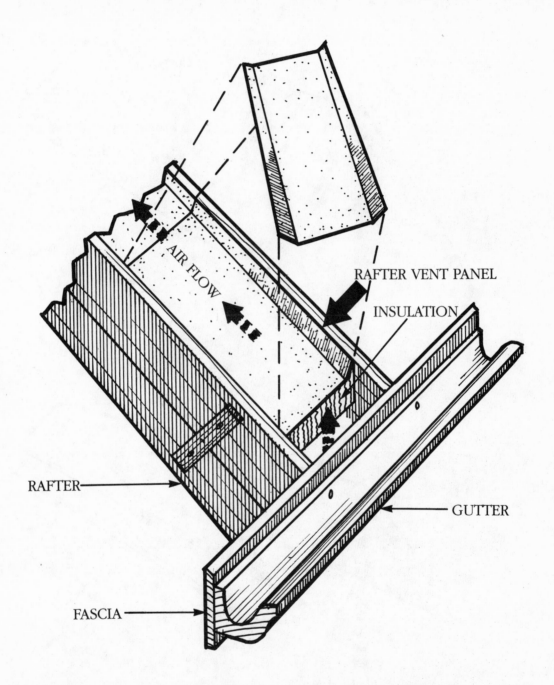

RAFTER VENT PANEL

INSULATION

AIR FLOW

RAFTER

GUTTER

FASCIA

Rafter venting, most essential in cathedral ceilings, is easily and inexpensively accomplished by using preformed foam units laid in on top of the rafter insulation. They are laid up from eaves to ridge, creating a channel of air about 1 inch deep by the width of the rafter bay. Insulation contractors are very familiar with this product, but you should tell your builder that it's what you want in your cathedral ceiling.

Insulation

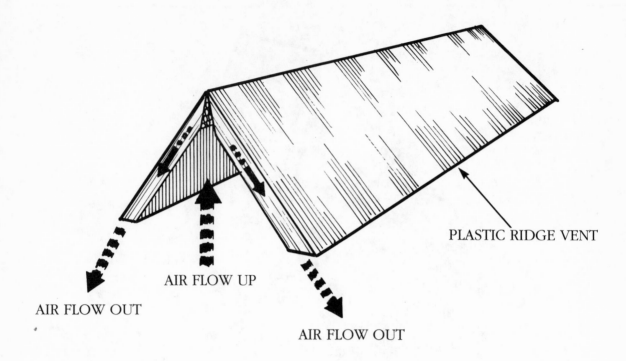

PLASTIC RIDGE VENT

AIR FLOW UP

AIR FLOW OUT

AIR FLOW OUT

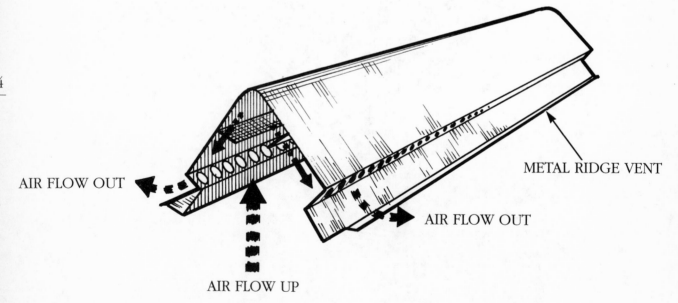

AIR FLOW OUT

METAL RIDGE VENT

AIR FLOW OUT

AIR FLOW UP

There are plastic and metal ridge vents. They all function the same way: vented air is naturally forced up to the top of the vent, exhausting down and out through the venting holes.

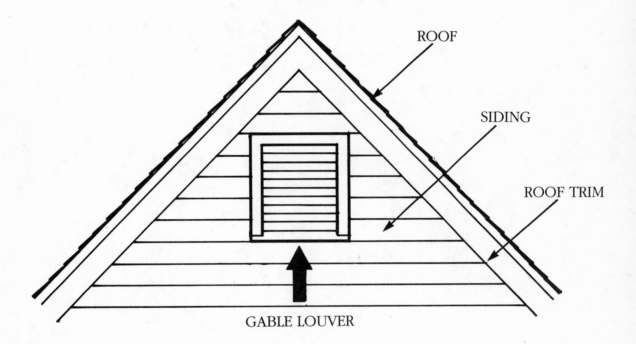

ROOF

SIDING

ROOF TRIM

GABLE LOUVER

Gable louvers can be wood or metal. They work best when they are as close to the ridge as possible, are at each end of the house, and are the same size at each end of the house.

The thing to insist on here is size, and the rule of thumb is the same as it is if you're using rafter ventilation: 1 square foot of venting for every 150 square feet of ceiling in the rooms below or 1 square foot of venting for every 300 square feet of ceiling if there's a vapor barrier in place. If a screen mesh is used, add 100 percent. Local building codes may call for different sizes, but what I have used has worked well for me.

Exterior Trim

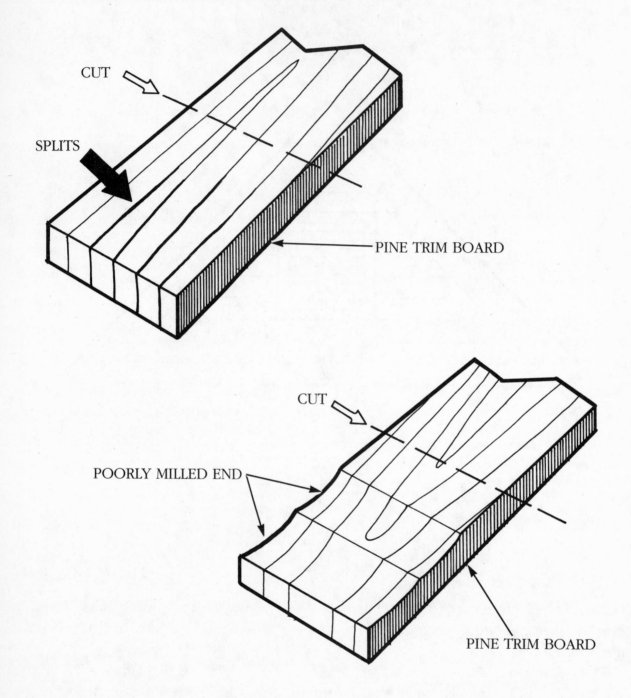

CUT

SPLITS

PINE TRIM BOARD

CUT

POORLY MILLED END

PINE TRIM BOARD

Many trim boards shipped out of the mill are either split or poorly milled. In both cases the bad ends should be cut off. I've seen expensive houses with defective trim boards like these. It is an indication of the builder's attitude. A careful builder will cut off these ends.

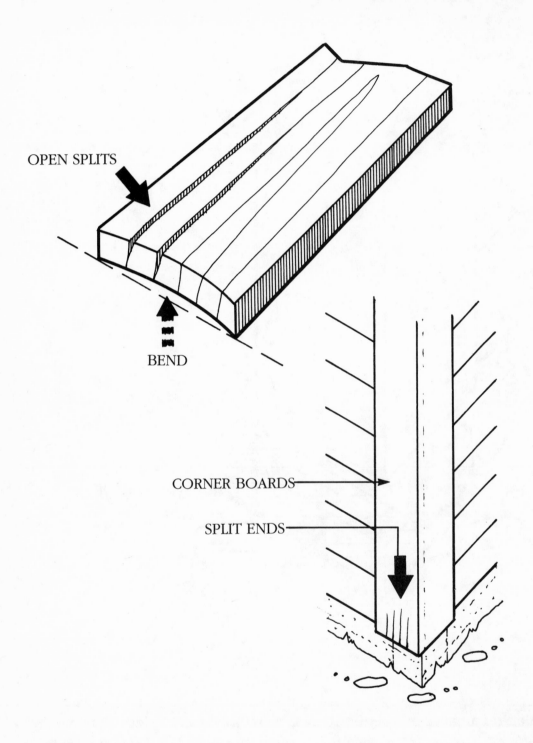

OPEN SPLITS

BEND

CORNER BOARDS

SPLIT ENDS

Split ends are often not easy to see, but bending the board will open them up. I always square the end of a trim board. If the end has a split, pieces will fall away as I cut. Splits in trim are to be avoided because they only get worse with age, and they are an invitation to rot, particularly when the splits are near the ground or where water collects, such as at corner boards and window and door trim.

Exterior Trim

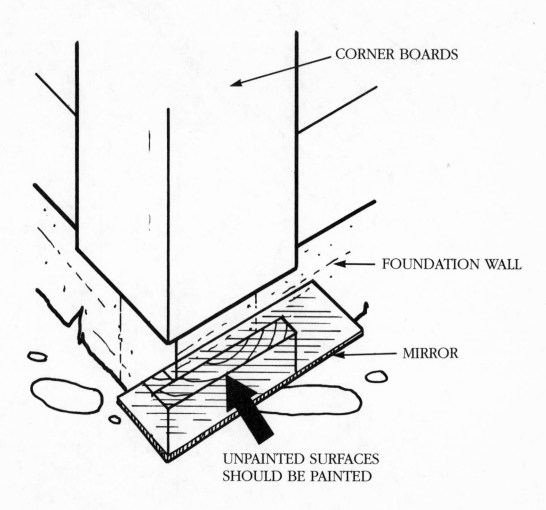

CORNER BOARDS

FOUNDATION WALL

MIRROR

UNPAINTED SURFACES
SHOULD BE PAINTED

Check to see that *all* surfaces of exterior trim are painted or stained, including the surfaces that won't be seen. One surface that is often overlooked is the bottom edge of corner boards. Checking the underside with a mirror is helpful when it's difficult to get an eyeball on it. It is most important to paint the bottom-edge end grain because unsealed end grain sucks water in like a sponge, and the end result will be rot.

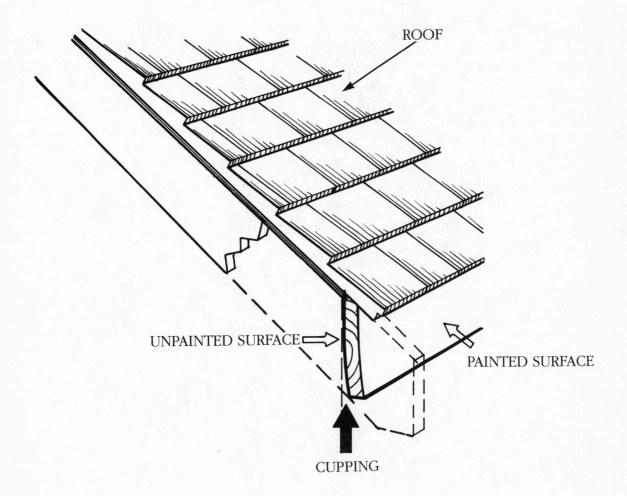

ROOF

UNPAINTED SURFACE ⇨

PAINTED SURFACE

CUPPING

The back side of flat trim boards must be painted to prevent cupping. Unpainted boards, even when they're not directly exposed to the weather, will absorb moisture, then swell and cup.

Once the trim is in place, you can't tell if the backside has been painted, but if during construction you see that the trim in place is not yet painted, you can be sure that the back hasn't been either. I wouldn't dream of putting up trim that wasn't primed front and back for protection from sun and rain. In fact, when trim gets delivered to my jobs, it's immediately put under cover, and it gets primed fast.

Exterior Trim

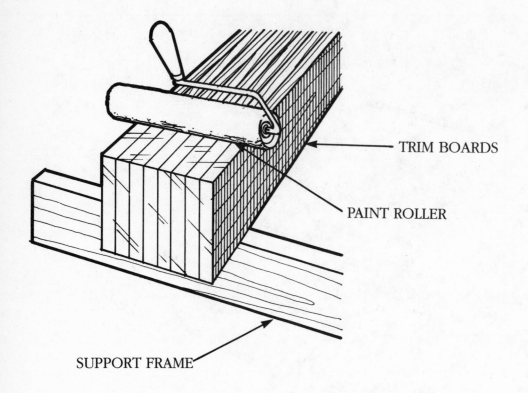

TRIM BOARDS

PAINT ROLLER

SUPPORT FRAME

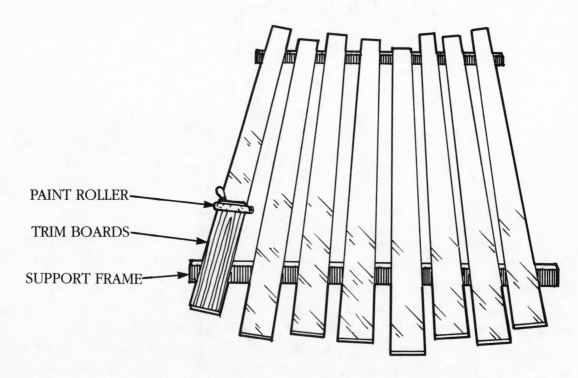

PAINT ROLLER

TRIM BOARDS

SUPPORT FRAME

This is a job you can offer to do for your builder. It's quick and easy, and handling it yourself is a sure way to know that your trim is primed front and back. One coat is enough.

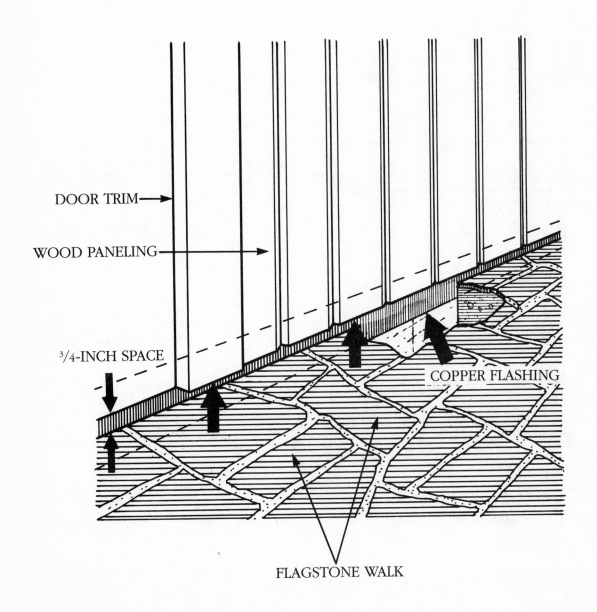

DOOR TRIM

WOOD PANELING

3/4-INCH SPACE

COPPER FLASHING

FLAGSTONE WALK

Make sure that exterior wood trim is kept off masonry floors in places like entry-ways and breezeways. When wood trim is installed directly on concrete or stone, it won't get a chance to dry out, nor can it be painted later to prevent water absorption. The areas where masonry meets wood can't be repaired easily and must be flashed, preferably with long-lasting copper. When I've had to, I've trimmed the bottoms of boards that were hard against a masonry floor by using a hand-held circular saw. I set the blade to cut just shy of reaching the flashing behind the trim and finish the cut using a sharp utility knife and chisel.

Exterior Trim

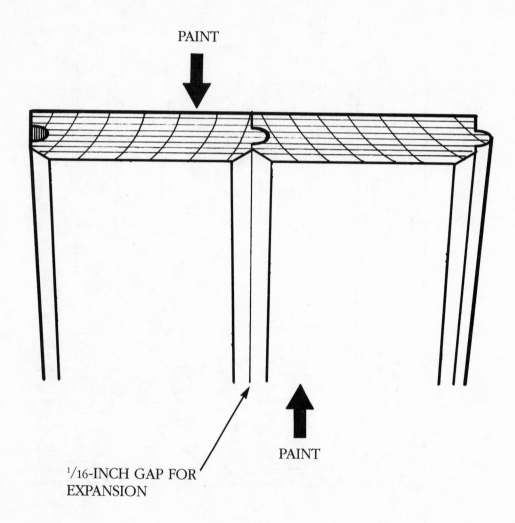

PAINT

PAINT

1/16-INCH GAP FOR
EXPANSION

You'll sometimes find an exterior door or gate made up of 1x6 or 1x8 boards. Be sure they've all been primed before they're put together, or expansion and contraction across their grain will lead to disaster. Even primed and painted, they'll swell and shrink, so the boards should be spaced about 1/16 inch apart. These expansion joints and at least three coats of paint will keep the boards from buckling and the door or gate from jamming in its frame.

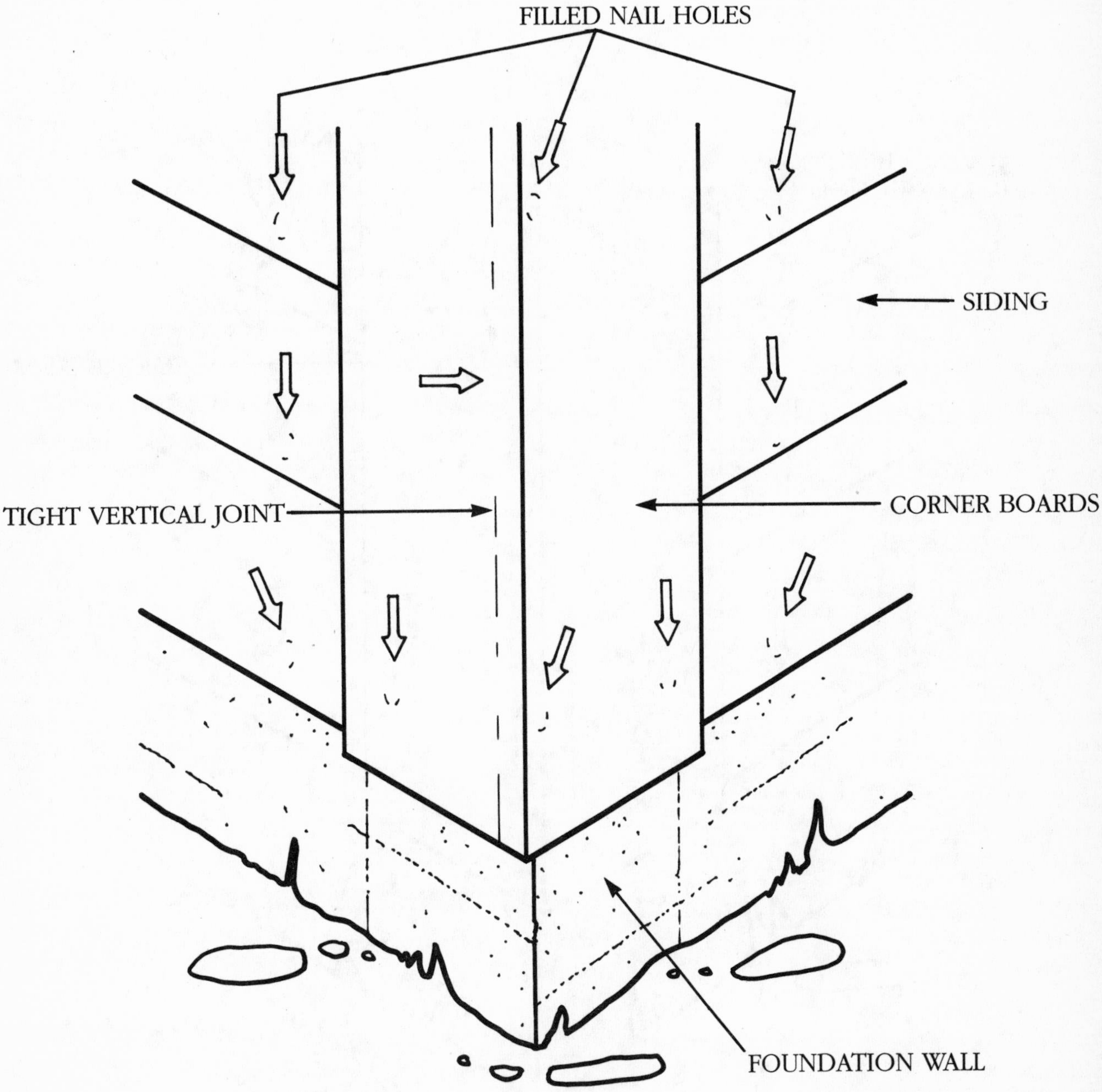

FILLED NAIL HOLES

SIDING

TIGHT VERTICAL JOINT

CORNER BOARDS

43

FOUNDATION WALL

Look to see if nails are set and filled in painted exterior wood trim. Setting nails with a nailset pulls the joints together, and filling, done properly, will make the nailing spots very difficult to find. You'll appreciate this the first time you scrape and repaint your house. It's nasty to scrape trim that has not had the nails set. Scraping over the nail head will remove the galvanized coating and invites rust.

Exterior Trim

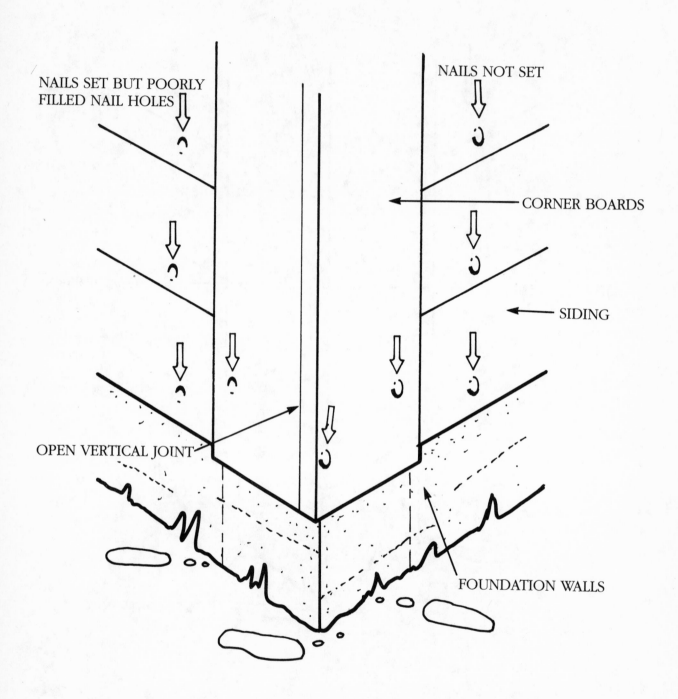

NAILS SET BUT POORLY FILLED NAIL HOLES

NAILS NOT SET

CORNER BOARDS

SIDING

OPEN VERTICAL JOINT

FOUNDATION WALLS

Unfortunately, you'll often find these conditions. Poorly done nailing, aside from not pulling the joints together, looks bad. In this drawing the nails on the right are not set, and they show up as bumps. The nails on the left side are set, but the holes are poorly filled, forming a depression or crater.

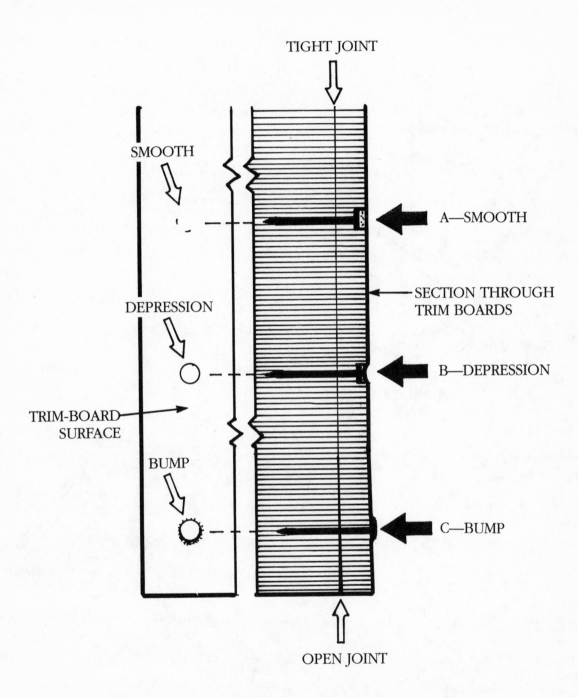

Here's how three nailing conditions look on the surface.

Nail "A" is set and filled properly and is hardly noticeable. The joint is tight.

Nail "B" is set but carelessly filled, forming a depression. The joint is tight.

Nail "C" is not set, and it shows as a bump on the surface. The joint is not tight.

Exterior Trim

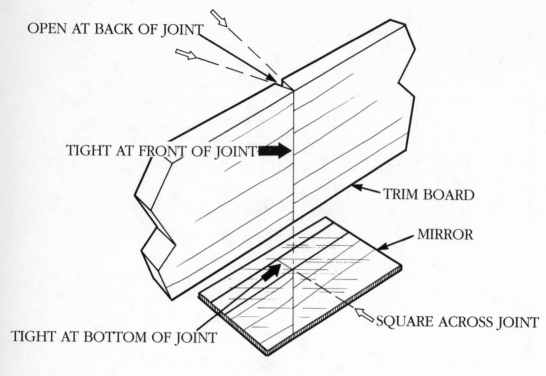

OPEN AT BACK OF JOINT

TIGHT AT FRONT OF JOINT

TRIM BOARD

MIRROR

TIGHT AT BOTTOM OF JOINT

SQUARE ACROSS JOINT

SQUARE-CUT JOINT

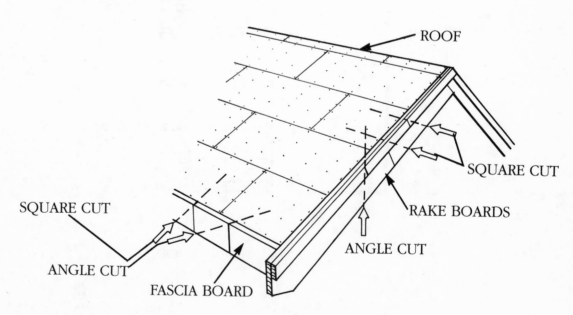

ROOF

SQUARE CUT

SQUARE CUT

RAKE BOARDS

ANGLE CUT

ANGLE CUT

FASCIA BOARD

Not many builders know how to make tight, long-lasting, square-cut exterior trim joints. It's quick, it's easy, and it will look good for as long as the house stands. The trick is to relieve the back edge of the joint by angling the cut slightly while keeping a true vertical front cut. Where the edge of the joint is visible, such as at the bottom edge of the rake board, the cut must return to square. It's not a difficult or time-consuming cut, and it's easy to trim to length for a tight fit using a block plane.

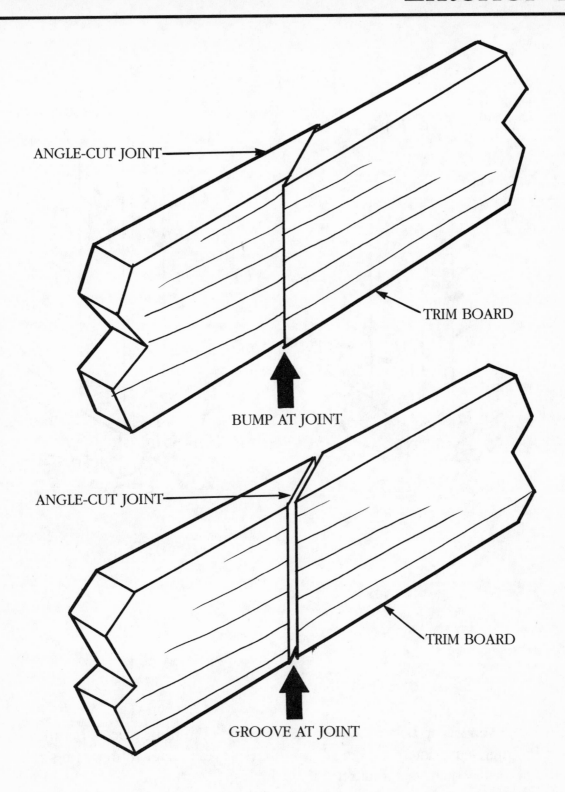

ANGLE-CUT JOINT

TRIM BOARD

BUMP AT JOINT

ANGLE-CUT JOINT

TRIM BOARD

GROOVE AT JOINT

Many builders use an angle-cut joint, thinking it's a better joint. I used to be one of those builders. Here are two reasons not to use such a joint: First, it's difficult to get a good fit. Second, the joint is not stable, and each board can slide back and forth, creating a bump or a depression at the joint.

Exterior Trim

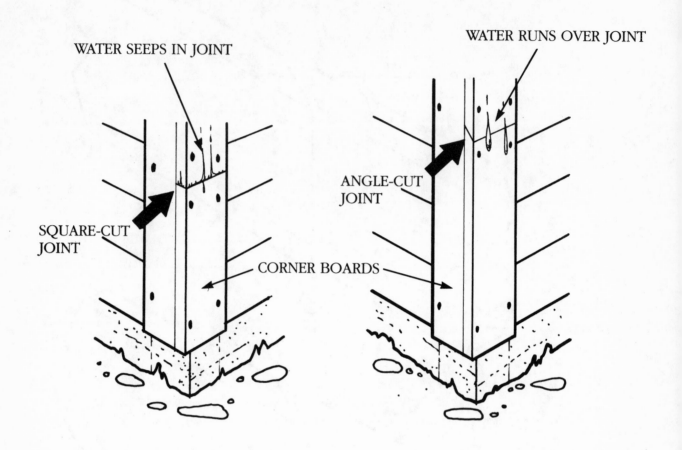

WATER SEEPS IN JOINT

WATER RUNS OVER JOINT

SQUARE-CUT JOINT

ANGLE-CUT JOINT

CORNER BOARDS

I prefer the quicker, easier, better-looking square-cut joint in most places, but there is a place for angle-cut joints. On vertical trim, they prevent water from getting into the joint, whereas a square-cut joint attracts water.

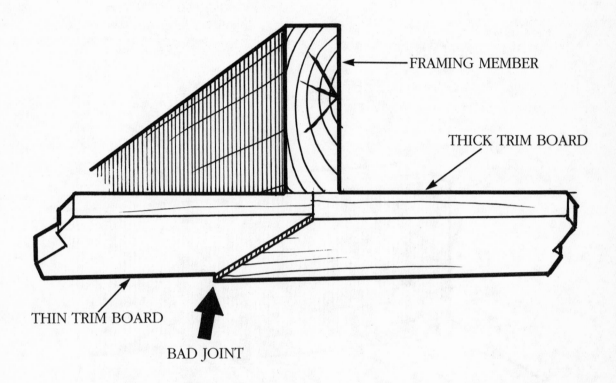

FRAMING MEMBER

THICK TRIM BOARD

THIN TRIM BOARD

BAD JOINT

Here's something to look for: trim boards not in the same plane on the surface. You can't rely on trim stock from the lumberyard to be the same thickness from board to board, or even from one end of the same board to the other. A careless carpenter will ignore the difference, and the end result will be an uneven surface.

Exterior Trim

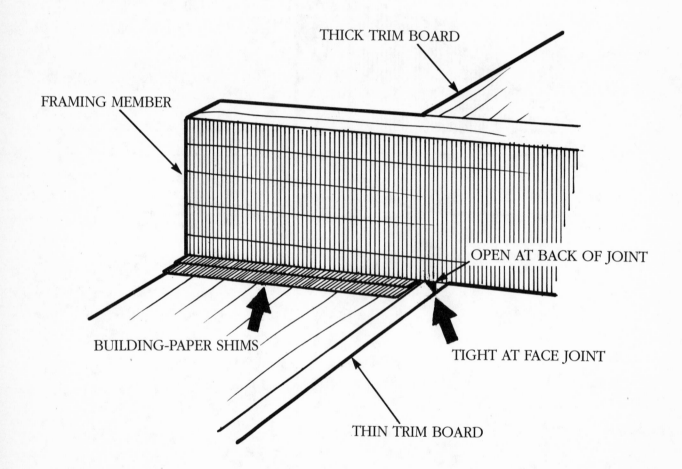

THICK TRIM BOARD

FRAMING MEMBER

OPEN AT BACK OF JOINT

BUILDING-PAPER SHIMS

TIGHT AT FACE JOINT

THIN TRIM BOARD

I plane the back side of the higher board when it's thicker than it should be, or shim the thin board if it's too thin. Strips of building paper (tar paper) make good shim stock.

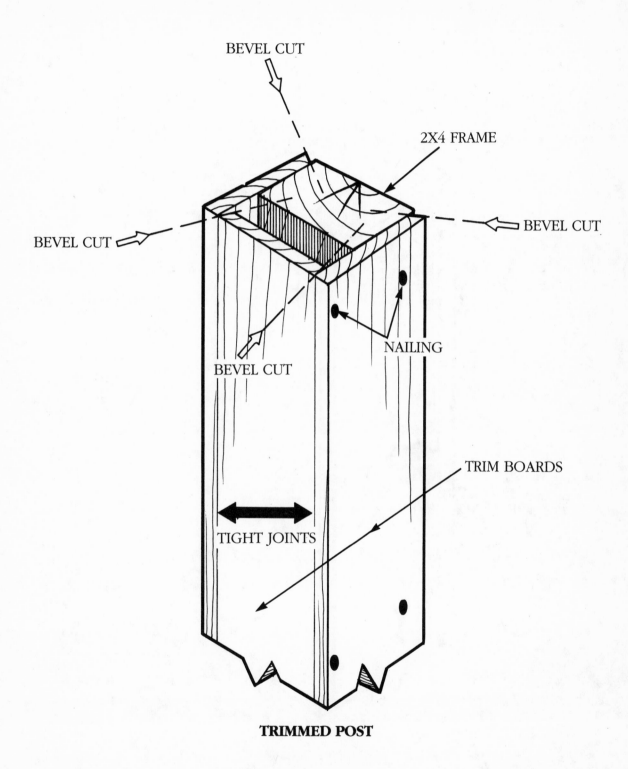

TRIMMED POST

Good joints indicate good craftsmanship, and they are easier to make than bad ones because good joints go together with less effort than bad joints. Relieving the back, unseen edge of a joint is the trick. It can be done quickly by bevel-cutting all the trim stock joints in one session on a table saw.

51

Exterior Trim

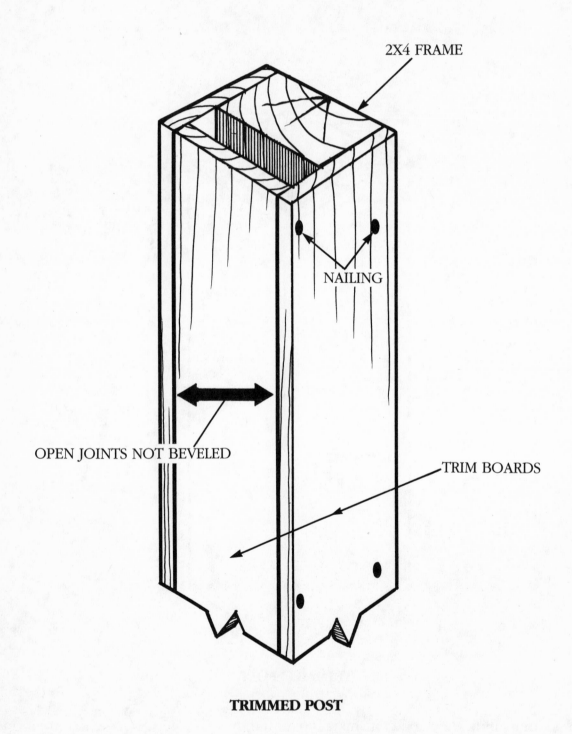

2X4 FRAME

NAILING

OPEN JOINTS NOT BEVELED

TRIM BOARDS

TRIMMED POST

This is what happens when boards are not beveled. The joints are open, and it's a struggle to nail them together. It's a sign of poor craftsmanship.

Blocking for Exterior Nailing

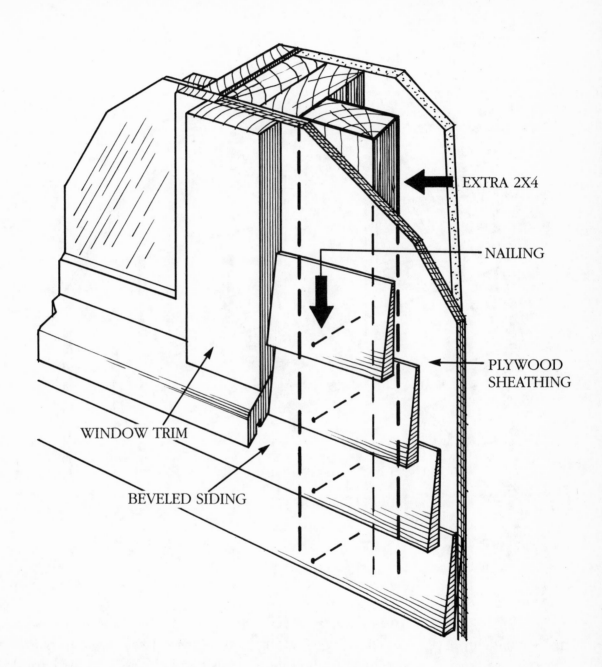

EXTRA 2X4

NAILING

PLYWOOD
SHEATHING

WINDOW TRIM

BEVELED SIDING

You really need this extra 2x4 if you want the siding nails to hold the siding securely in place. Nailing only into the plywood sheathing simply will not do the job. This is another case where you have to tell your builder what you want and why you want it.

Beveled siding must be nailed at each stud, but what happens at doors and windows and corners? In every new house with beveled siding that I have checked out in my neighborhood, these extra 2x4s at doors, windows, and corners are missing, and the nails poke through the plywood sheathing. They may be holding for now, but they won't be in a few years.

Blocking for Exterior Nailing

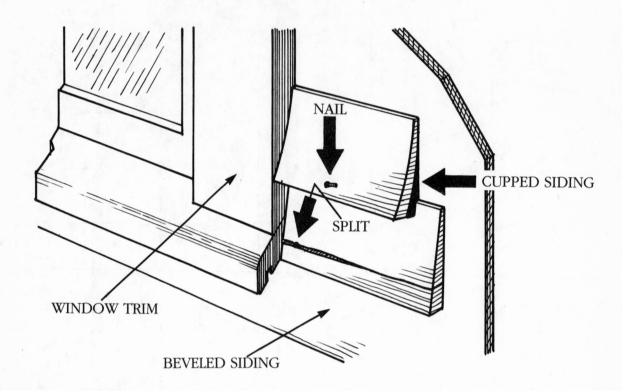

NAIL

CUPPED SIDING

SPLIT

WINDOW TRIM

BEVELED SIDING

This is what can happen when there is nothing but plywood sheathing to nail into. Nails will "walk out" as the siding cups. Ringed nails can help here. Splits happen when the nails are driven too close to the end of the board. With blocking in place, the carpenter can nail back from the end of the trim, and splitting can be eliminated.

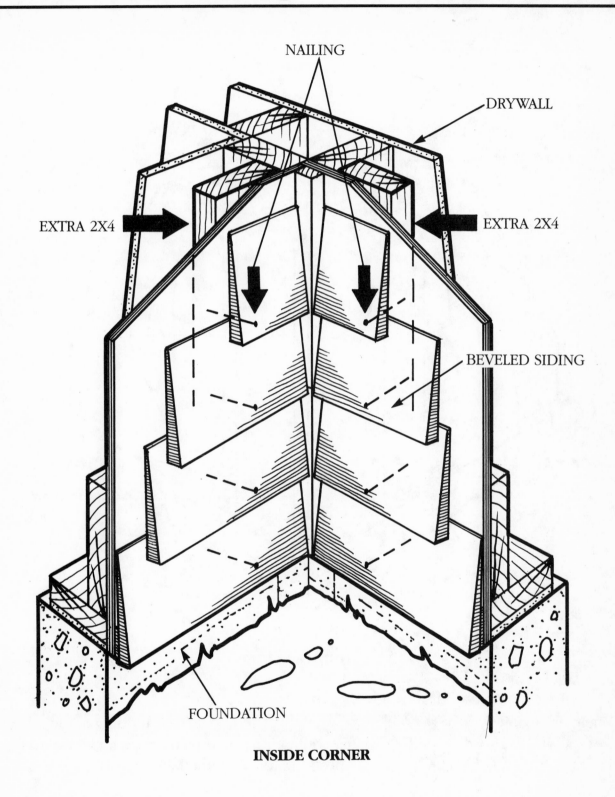

NAILING

DRYWALL

EXTRA 2X4

EXTRA 2X4

BEVELED SIDING

FOUNDATION

INSIDE CORNER

Extra 2x4s are required at inside corners, too—not by building codes, but for better building practices. If you want your siding to stay in place, make sure it's nailed securely.

Blocking for Exterior Nailing

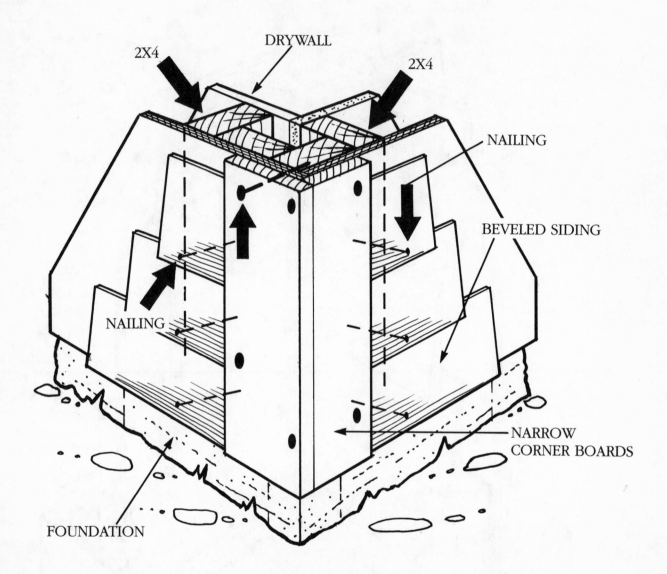

DRYWALL

2X4

2X4

NAILING

BEVELED SIDING

NAILING

NARROW
CORNER BOARDS

FOUNDATION

OUTSIDE CORNER

There are many ways to build exterior walls at the corners. The studding at the corner shown here works well for average-width corner boards because there are good nailing surfaces *behind* the plywood sheathing for securing the corner boards and the siding.

Blocking for Exterior Nailing

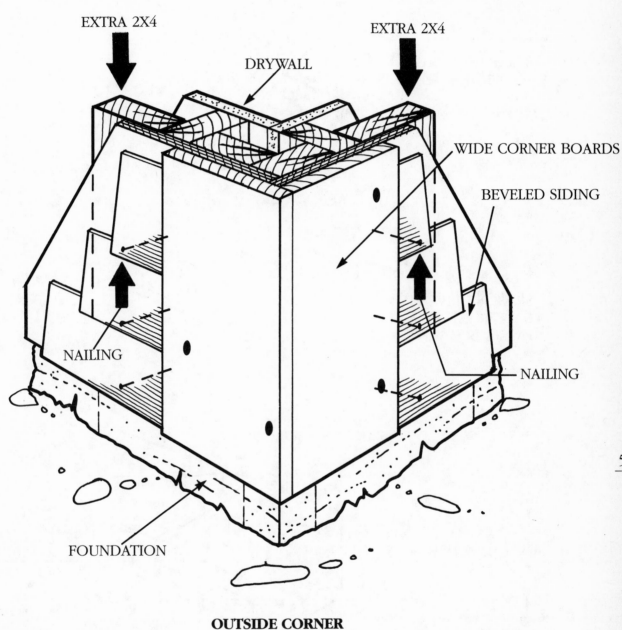

EXTRA 2X4

EXTRA 2X4

DRYWALL

WIDE CORNER BOARDS

BEVELED SIDING

NAILING

NAILING

FOUNDATION

OUTSIDE CORNER

In this case, where wide corner boards are used (strictly a design preference), extra 2x4s are necessary.

Gutters

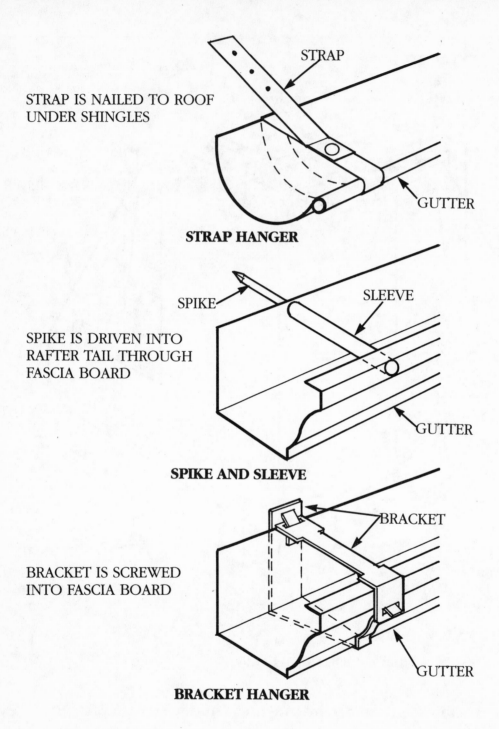

STRAP

STRAP IS NAILED TO ROOF
UNDER SHINGLES

GUTTER

STRAP HANGER

SPIKE

SLEEVE

SPIKE IS DRIVEN INTO
RAFTER TAIL THROUGH
FASCIA BOARD

GUTTER

SPIKE AND SLEEVE

BRACKET

BRACKET IS SCREWED
INTO FASCIA BOARD

GUTTER

BRACKET HANGER

The function of a gutter is to catch rain or snow-melt that flows off the roof. It carries the water to downspouts, which drain it off onto the ground. Gutters—whether they are made of wood, copper, galvanized steel, vinyl, or aluminum—carry loads (water, ice, snow). Make sure they are fastened securely in place. I nail wood gutters every 32 inches into a framing member. Copper, aluminum, vinyl, and galvanized steel should also be securely fastened every 32 inches.

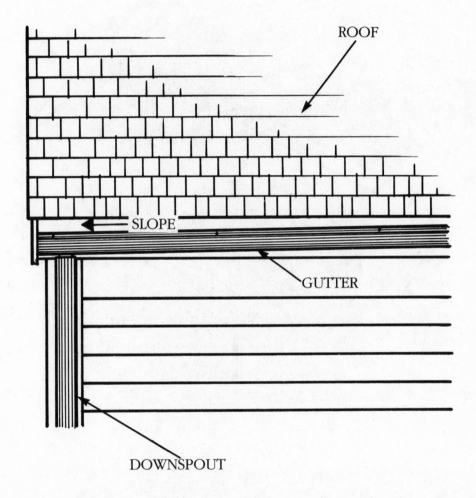

Check to see if a gutter is sloped properly by pouring a bucket of water into its high point. The water should run smoothly to the downspouts. There should be no water standing in the gutter.

Gutters

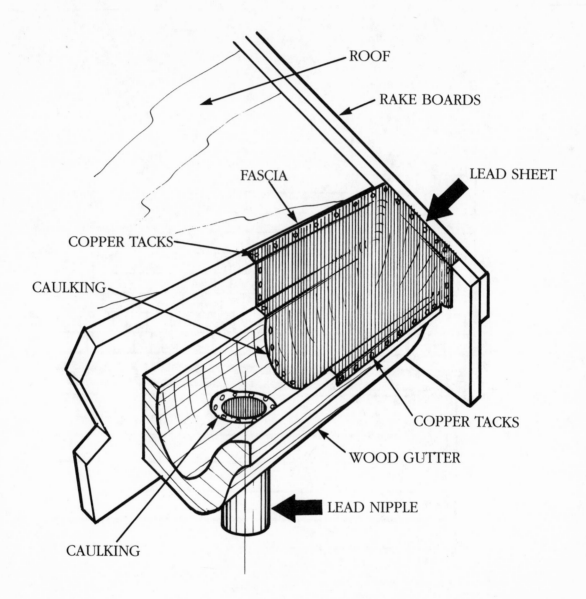

ROOF

RAKE BOARDS

FASCIA

LEAD SHEET

COPPER TACKS

CAULKING

COPPER TACKS

WOOD GUTTER

LEAD NIPPLE

CAULKING

Wood gutters are pretty much regional and I like them; but they are dying out, even on Cape Cod. If you have them or are planning to use wood gutters, make sure they are properly flashed at the ends. That's a prime spot for rot, not only in the gutter but in the surrounding wood as well. Flashing takes a fairly large piece of lead, many copper tacks, and lots of caulking. It's not an easy job, but by patiently tapping the lead to shape it in place (using the butt end of a rubber-handled hammer), I can complete one gutter end in about forty-five minutes.

I like to use a lead nipple at the downspout, and it must be well caulked and tacked. This flashing is an important job, so ask to have it done right and check to make sure it was done right. I've had to repair rotted gutter ends, and it's always the skimpy 3-inch strip of lead flashing that has failed.

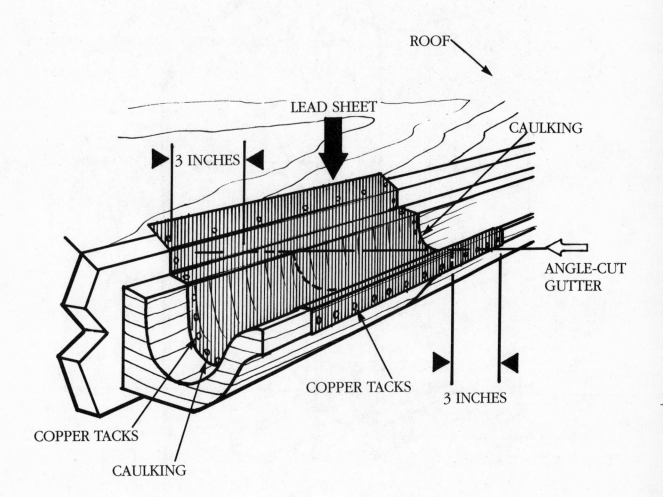

ROOF

LEAD SHEET

CAULKING

◄ 3 INCHES ◄

ANGLE-CUT
GUTTER

COPPER TACKS

3 INCHES

COPPER TACKS

CAULKING

The mid-span gutter joint, which is angle-cut from front to back, is easily covered
with a piece of sheet lead. Using a thin strip of lead over the joint might protect the
joint for a year or so, but for long-lasting protection it's better to be generous with
the lead, caulking, and tacks. This is about a twenty-minute job. Again, ask for it and
make sure you get it.

Windows and Exterior Doors

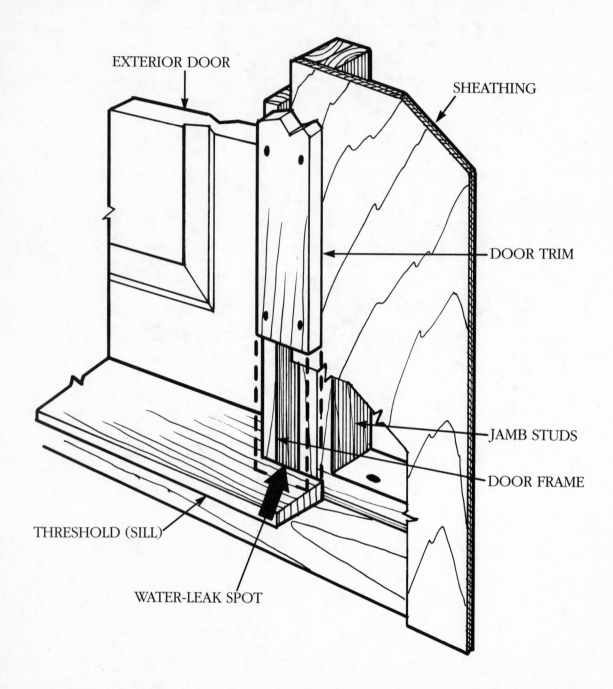

EXTERIOR DOOR

SHEATHING

DOOR TRIM

JAMB STUDS

DOOR FRAME

THRESHOLD (SILL)

WATER-LEAK SPOT

Window and door leaks occur most often between the door or window frame and the jamb studs at the *sill*. The water gets there through the joint where the siding butts against the trim.

Caulking is a temporary fix and looks bad. I have repaired many leaking and damaged thresholds. When the door is on the second floor, the leak shows itself in the ceiling below. Often the leak will show up a few feet away from its source because water will flow along a horizontal framing member for a way before dropping vertically. I fixed such a threshold leak for a puzzled homeowner who had water dripping from the middle of the living room ceiling.

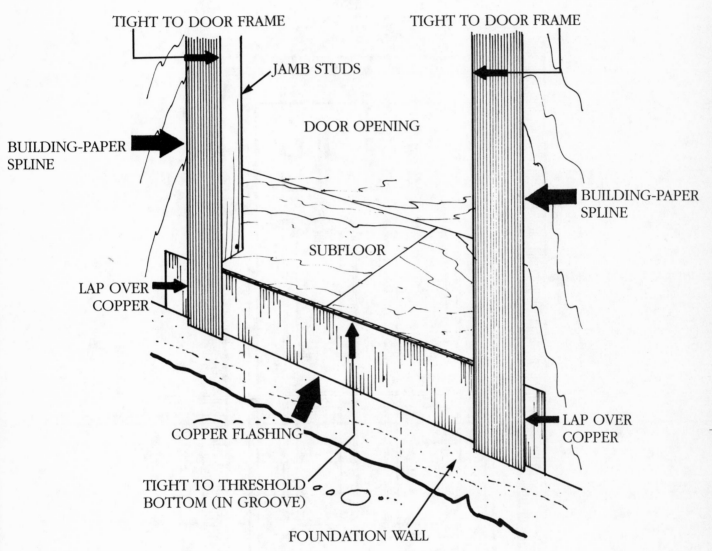

TIGHT TO DOOR FRAME

TIGHT TO DOOR FRAME

JAMB STUDS

DOOR OPENING

BUILDING-PAPER
SPLINE

BUILDING-PAPER
SPLINE

SUBFLOOR

LAP OVER
COPPER

LAP OVER
COPPER

COPPER FLASHING

TIGHT TO THRESHOLD
BOTTOM (IN GROOVE)

FOUNDATION WALL

63

The common errors here are not getting the metal flashing up into a groove in the bottom of the threshold and not running the building-paper splines, at each side of the door, over the metal threshold flashing. Without the splines, water will get behind the threshold flashing and into the room below.

Exterior Door Flashing

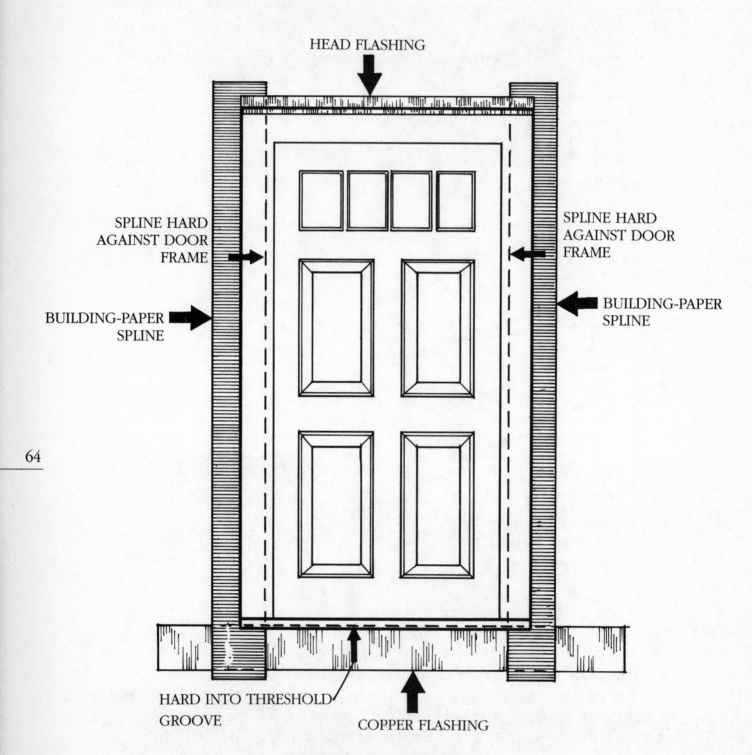

HEAD FLASHING

SPLINE HARD AGAINST DOOR FRAME

SPLINE HARD AGAINST DOOR FRAME

BUILDING-PAPER SPLINE

BUILDING-PAPER SPLINE

HARD INTO THRESHOLD GROOVE

COPPER FLASHING

EXTERIOR DOOR FLASHING

Make sure your door flashing looks like this.

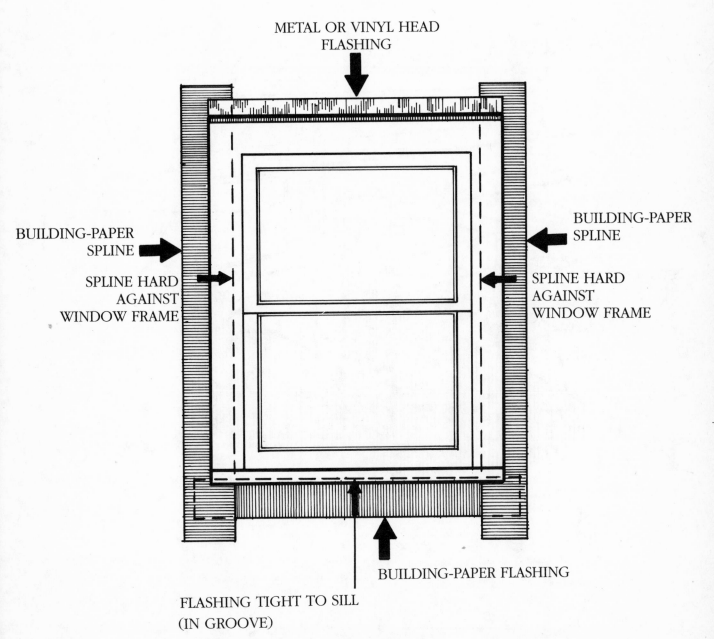

WINDOW FLASHING

Make sure your window flashing looks like this. In addition to the spline running over the paper sill flashing, the section of spline below the sill should run over the top of a siding course. This will divert water to the surface of the siding.

65

Window Flashing

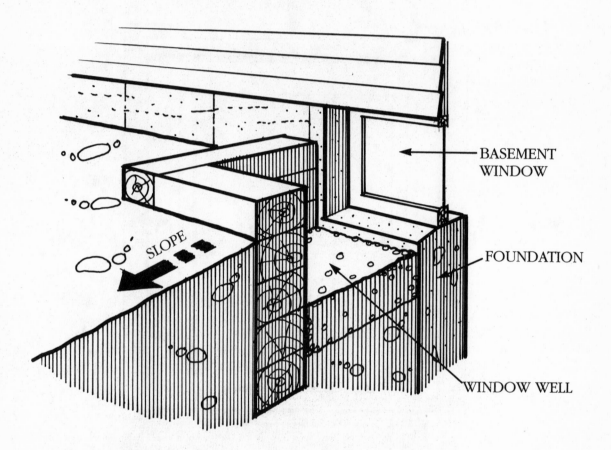

BASEMENT WINDOW

FOUNDATION

WINDOW WELL

SLOPE

Often, a lot of water enters a house's basement through a window well. Check to see that the ground surface is sloped away from such wells.

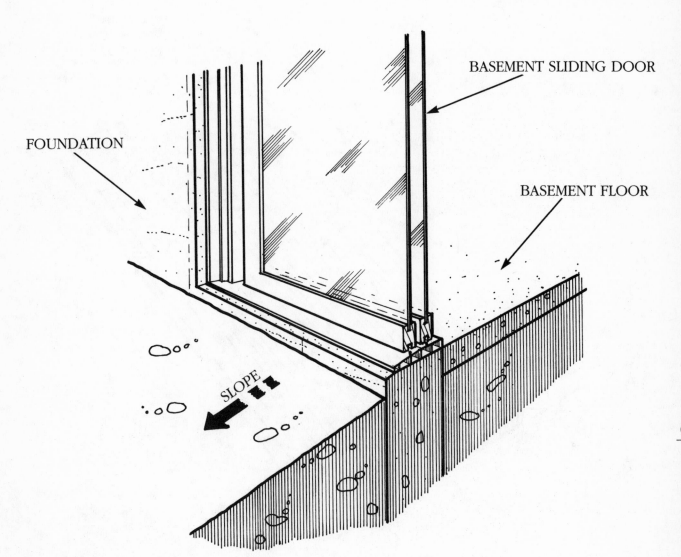

FOUNDATION

BASEMENT SLIDING DOOR

BASEMENT FLOOR

SLOPE

A basement sliding door is another spot where water can enter the house. Again, check to see that the grade is sloped away from the door.

Roofing

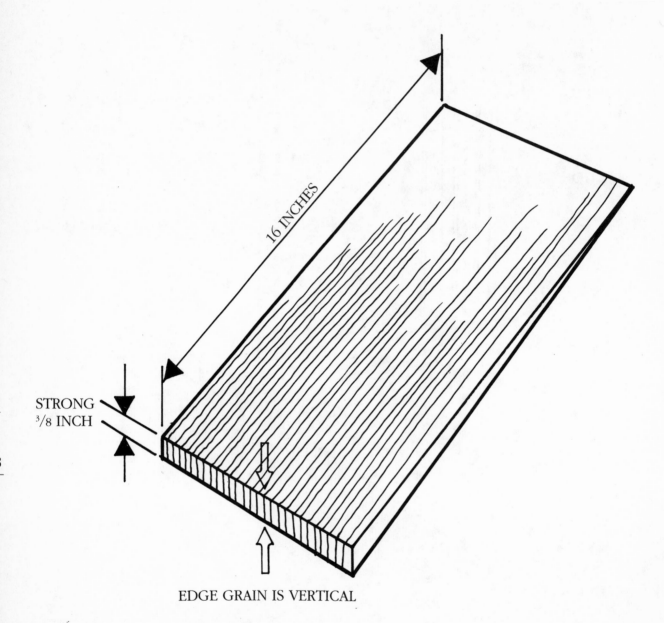

16 INCHES

STRONG
³/₈ INCH

EDGE GRAIN IS VERTICAL

I've installed a lot of wood-shingle roofs, and I know it's not smart to skimp on quality material here. Roofing is a labor-intensive job, so use the best—#1 red cedar. The #1 grade is 100 percent clear and edge grain (it won't soak up water like end grain). On 16-inch #1 shingles, the butts (the thick end of the shingle) are a strong ³/₈-inch thick (18-inch and 24-inch shingles have thicker butts).

I have seen builders use white cedar shingles on roofs, but the whites lack the natural oils of the red cedars, so their life expectancy is half that of the reds.

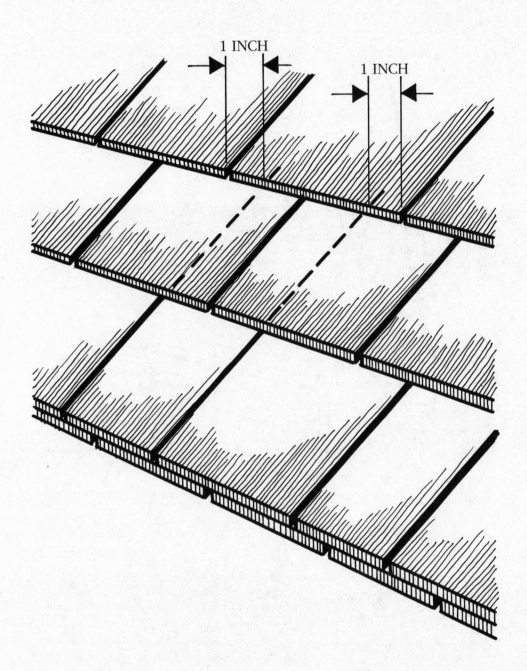

1 INCH   1 INCH

When I do a wood roof, I make sure the joints of every other course of shingles do not line up. I offset them by at least an inch. If they do line up, and if the middle course shingle splits at the same joint line as the shingle above or the shingle below (weeks, months, or years from the time of installation), the resulting crack will be open to the roofing underneath—and a roof leak is born.

Roofing

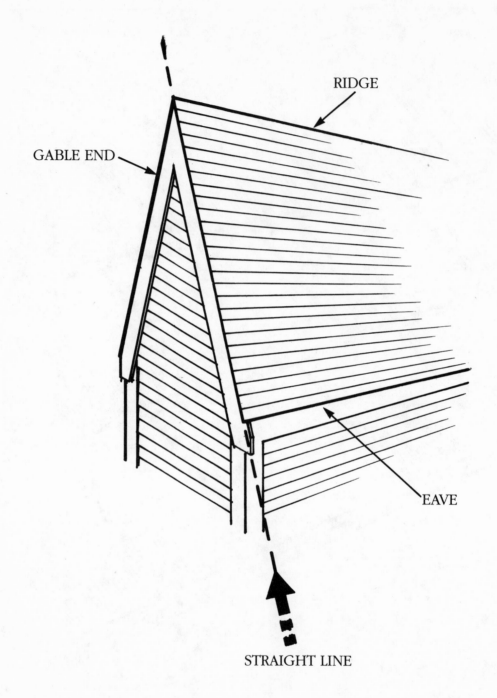

RIDGE

GABLE END

EAVE

STRAIGHT LINE

The crowning glory of a house is its roof, so it should be the best. The best asphalt roofing is the double-layer textured-look shingle with a 30-year warranty. All the major manufacturers make such a shingle. These textured shingles take more time to install, but they're worth the extra effort.

Check the gable ends. They should be straight as a string from eave to ridge: no lumps or bumps.

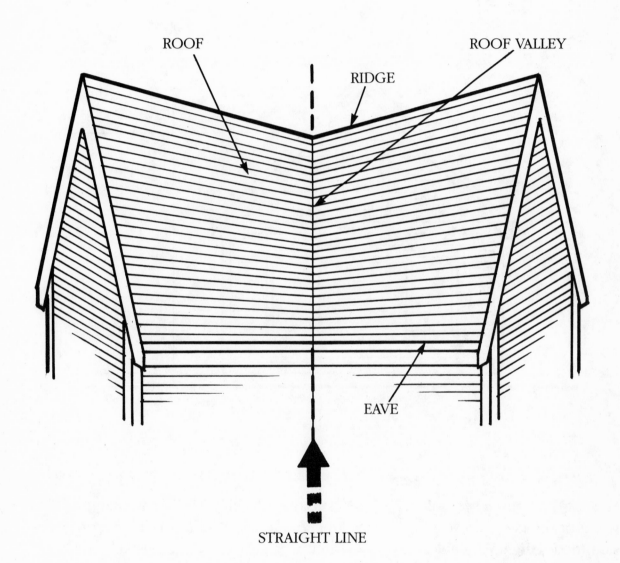

ROOF

ROOF VALLEY

RIDGE

EAVE

STRAIGHT LINE

Closed valleys, where shingles touch shingles, should be a straight line from eave to ridge. Open valleys, where a line of flashing separates the shingles of each roof plane, should be of copper.

Shingle Siding

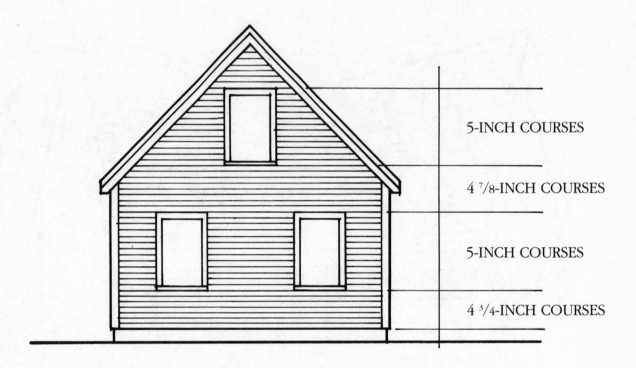

5-INCH COURSES

4 ⅞-INCH COURSES

5-INCH COURSES

4 ¾-INCH COURSES

Most of the houses I've built have white cedar siding, and I've found that the best-grade of shingle gives you the best-looking and longer-lasting job. I have on occasion tried "bargain" shingles, and I've regretted it every time. You usually get what you pay for, so use #1 clears. They look better, fit together better, and are easier to install with less waste. The butt is almost ⅜ inch thick.

Look for straight parallel courses.

Courses should have equal exposures when possible, but exposure changes of no more than ½ inch are okay when courses have to be adjusted. Good builders have to make adjustments to avoid narrow shingle courses above and below windows.

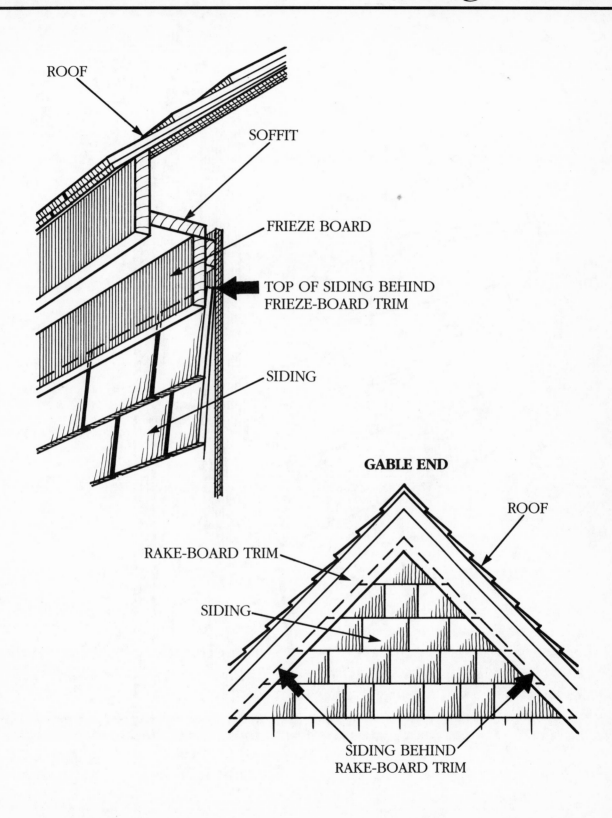

ROOF

SOFFIT

FRIEZE BOARD

TOP OF SIDING BEHIND
FRIEZE-BOARD TRIM

SIDING

GABLE END

ROOF

RAKE-BOARD TRIM

SIDING

SIDING BEHIND
RAKE-BOARD TRIM

73

I run the tops of shingles under the trim at window sills, under frieze boards, and under the rake-board trim at the gable ends. I've found that this prevents the shingles from splitting and falling out.

Shingle Siding

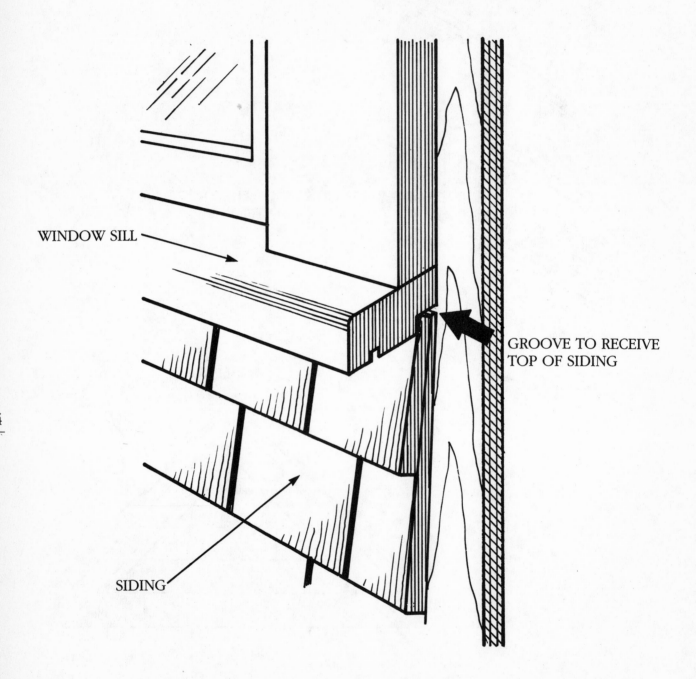

WINDOW SILL

GROOVE TO RECEIVE
TOP OF SIDING

SIDING

Under the windows, this technique requires cutting a groove in the bottom of the sill before installing the windows. Better builders will do this.

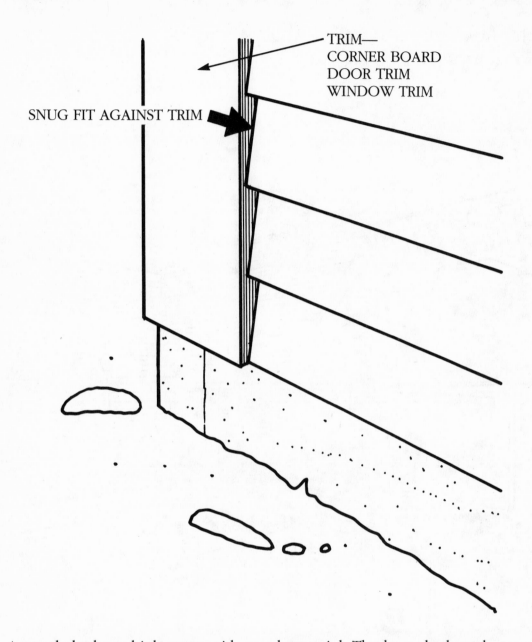

TRIM—
CORNER BOARD
DOOR TRIM
WINDOW TRIM

SNUG FIT AGAINST TRIM

A good clapboard job starts with good material. The best clapboards are clear, vertical-grain red cedar and redwood.

The careful builder will prime the front and back surfaces of all the clapboards before installing them. I prefer oil-base paint, because it wears well.

A good builder will adjust the courses so that a clapboard course starts at the window sill and the window head.

Check the fits at window and door casings and at corner boards. Each clapboard course should be snug against the trim. It's not difficult to get a good fit, but it does take some extra care. The careless builder will have many gaps, which he will then fill with caulking.

Inside the House

GOOD WORKMANSHIP INSIDE THE HOUSE
Where to Look and What to Look For

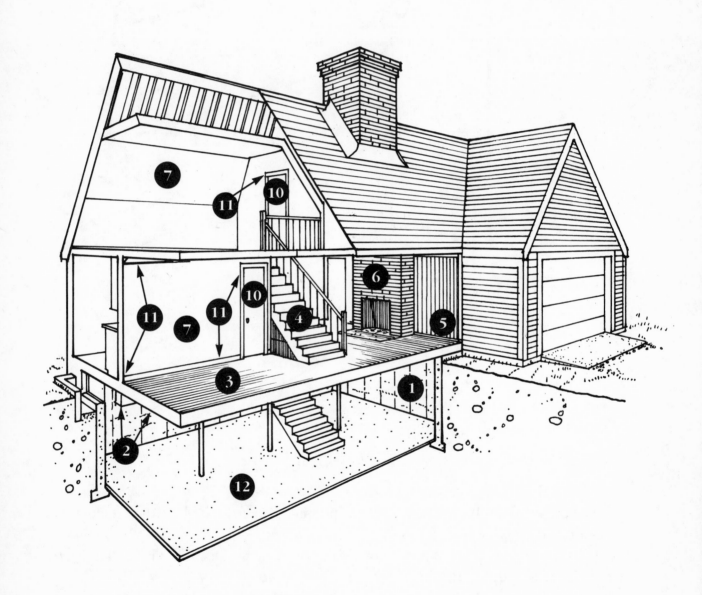

Inside the House

GOOD WORKMANSHIP INSIDE THE HOUSE
Where to Look and What to Look For

1. FOUNDATION WALLS: Smooth, crack-free with snap-tie holes filled.

2. STRUCTURAL FLOORS: Solid feel, indicating proper floor-joist size. Main floor beam (in basement) should be steel or "flush" wood beam.

3. WOOD FLOORS: Laid up tight, squeak-free, proper joint offset, scraped smooth in corners.

4. STAIRS: Solid feel with no squeaks. Solid newel post. Good joints where treads and risers meet wall. Smooth, well-anchored handrail with good joints. Balusters set into bottom of handrail.

5. SOLID WOOD PANELING: Good grain and color match. Tongues painted or stained.

6. FIREPLACE: Neat masonry work with no cracks or patches. Clean hearth with no water stains (water stains indicate chimney leaks).

7. WALLS: Neat drywall joints. No nail pops. No cracks over doors and windows.

8. COUNTERTOPS: Backsplash fitted tight to wall. Neat joints on counter surface.

9. CABINETS: European-style hinges and ball-bearing drawer glides are quality hardware. Drawers should operate smoothly with little side-to-side movement.

10. DOORS: Doors square in opening. Good trim joints at corners. Plumb. Door face touches door stops all around door opening. Doors painted or stained on all six surfaces (top, bottom, two faces, two edges). Even gap all around door jamb and edge of door. Nickle gap for paint (before painting), dime gap for stain (before staining). Smooth to the touch. Good quality hardware, neatly installed.

11. PAINTED OR STAINED TRIM: Good joints. Well nailed. Nailholes filled. All surfaces smooth to the touch. No repaired splits.

12. BASEMENT FLOOR: Dry, no water stains. Minimum floor cracks.

    MISC.: Well-anchored towel bars and grab bars. Softened corners on trim, especially on handrails. They should feel smooth to the touch.

Rule of Thumb for Sizing Floor Joists

Floor joists, which you can see in a basement's ceiling, are the wood framing members that support a house's floors. Sometimes builders use floor joists that meet the local building code but that are sized too small to support the floor properly. The result will be the kind of house in which the dishes in the cupboards rattle when you walk across the floor.

There are two quick ways to make sure a house's floor joists are properly sized. The first is to walk on the floor above; it should feel solid with just a *hint* of bounce.

The second way is to apply this rule of thumb:

1. Assume joists are space 16 inches on center (most are).
2. Treat measurements in feet as if they were in inches (don't convert—just treat 10 feet, say, as if it were 10 inches).
3. Measure the unsupported span of the joists (usually from the foundation wall to a main beam halfway across the basement).
4. Take ¹/₂ of the unsupported joist span (as if it were inches, remember), then add 2 inches.
5. The resulting number gives you the minimum depth for your floor joists.

Example:
Unsupported joist span = 15 feet
¹/₂ of 15 = 7 ¹/₂
7 ¹/₂ +2 = 9 ¹/₂
Converted to inches = 9 ¹/₂ inches

This is the depth you should be looking for in your floor joists. A 2x10 actually measures a little less than 9 ¹/₂ inches in depth. So if you use 2x10 floor joists, your floor might be soft or bouncy. Larger joists or closer joist spacing will produce a firmer floor.

This is only a general rule for a quick evaluation of existing joists. Factors such as lumber species and lumber grade affect the strength of lumber, which in turn affects the joist-span potential. Fir is stronger than spruce. Joist and plank select structural grade is stronger than joist and plank No. 3 grade.

Rule of Thumb for Sizing Floor Joists

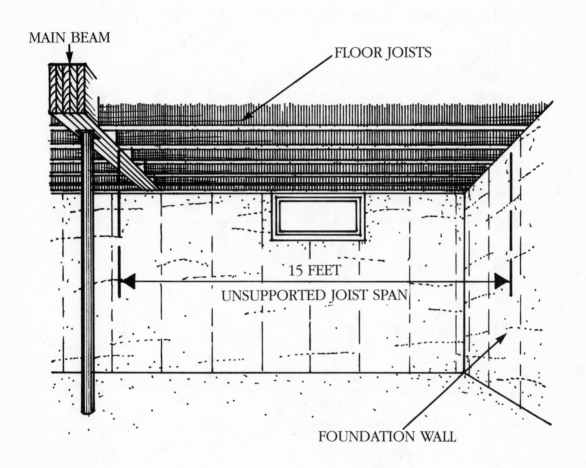

SIZING FLOOR JOISTS

Rule of Thumb for Sizing Floor Joists

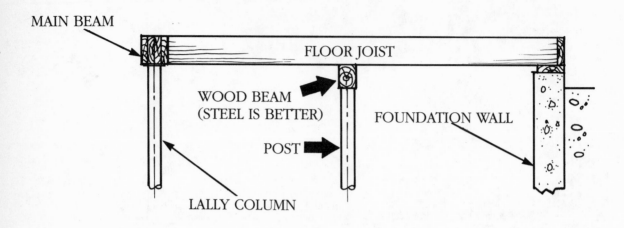

MAIN BEAM

FLOOR JOIST

WOOD BEAM
(STEEL IS BETTER)

POST

FOUNDATION WALL

LALLY COLUMN

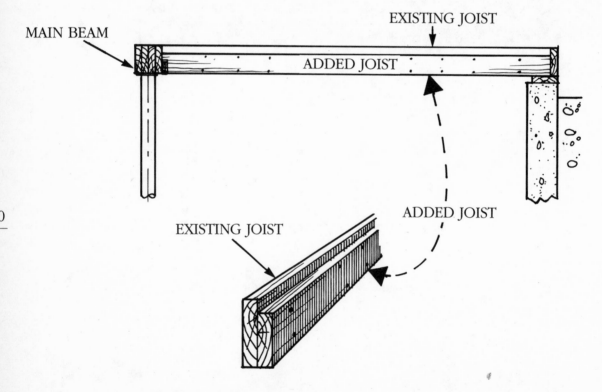

MAIN BEAM

EXISTING JOIST

ADDED JOIST

EXISTING JOIST

ADDED JOIST

A bouncy floor isn't dangerous, but it is annoying when the dishes rattle. I have remedied the situation in some houses by placing a secondary beam under the floor joists, halfway between the foundation wall and the main beam. This new beam doesn't have to be very big, because it's not carrying much of a load. A wood beam works, but it will probably have to be shimmed up snug to the joist bottoms as it shrinks.

Another solution is to stiffen each joist by adding a smaller joist to it on either side, well nailed. This system has the advantage of not requiring posts.

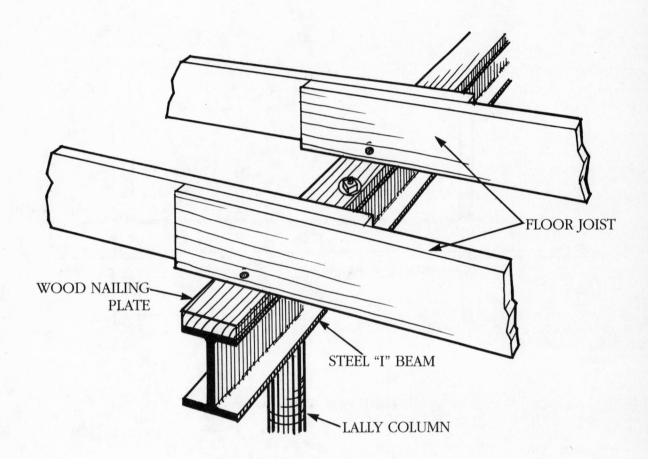

DROPPED "I" BEAM

This is the best and most common system for the main carrying beam, which supports the floor joists at mid-span between the foundation walls.

The steel beam is heavy, but it can be delivered right onto the foundation wall. Some suppliers will even set it place. When it is delivered onto the wall, it can be shoved over to the beam pockets without too much trouble. I did it alone with my first house. Once it's in place, a 2x6 nailing plate is bolted or power-nailed to its top surface.

Main Carrying Beam

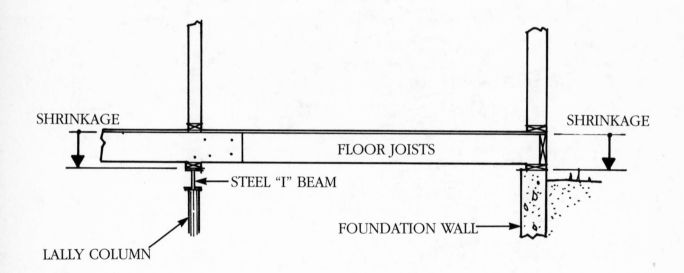

SHRINKAGE

SHRINKAGE

FLOOR JOISTS

STEEL "I" BEAM

FOUNDATION WALL

LALLY COLUMN

DROPPED "I" BEAM

The joists sit directly on the nailing plate at one end and on the foundation wall's mud sill on the other. Because these two elements are the same size, their shrinkage under the floor joists will be equal. The floor will remain level.

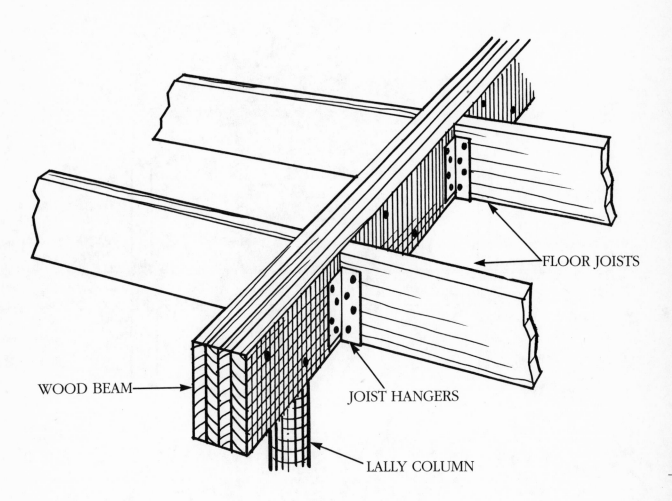

FLOOR JOISTS

WOOD BEAM

JOIST HANGERS

LALLY COLUMN

83

FLUSH WOOD BEAM

This system takes more time to build, but it's as good as the dropped "I" beam, and it saves headroom because the beam is up within the joist space rather than below it.

Main Carrying Beam

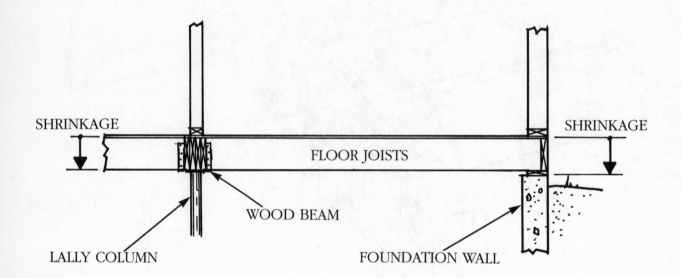

SHRINKAGE

SHRINKAGE

FLOOR JOISTS

WOOD BEAM

LALLY COLUMN

FOUNDATION WALL

FLUSH WOOD BEAM

In this system, there will be a little uneven shrinkage as the mud sill ages, but this is a minor factor when the sill is a 2x6.

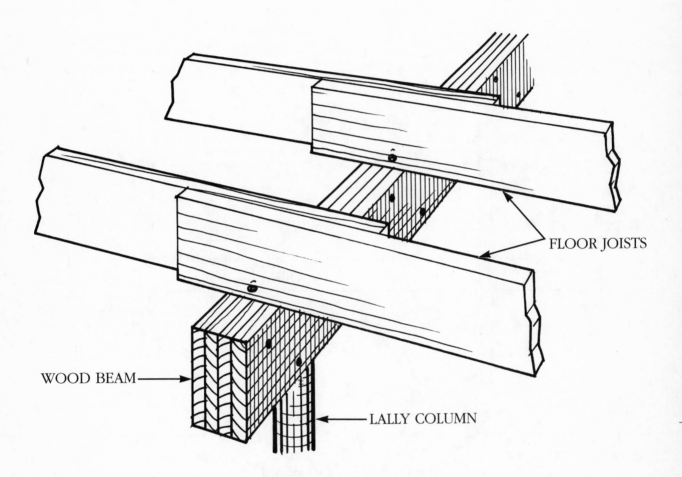

FLOOR JOISTS

WOOD BEAM

LALLY COLUMN

DROPPED WOOD BEAM

If you see this beam system in your house, expect trouble. This is the worst system, and one I never use.

Main Carrying Beam

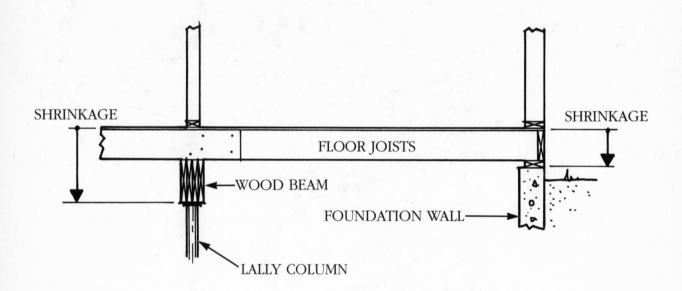

SHRINKAGE

SHRINKAGE

FLOOR JOISTS

WOOD BEAM

FOUNDATION WALL

LALLY COLUMN

DROPPED WOOD BEAM

The shrinkage problem under the floor joists is obvious here. The deeper the wood beam, the more the shrinkage difference. Using unseasoned lumber will make the problem even worse.

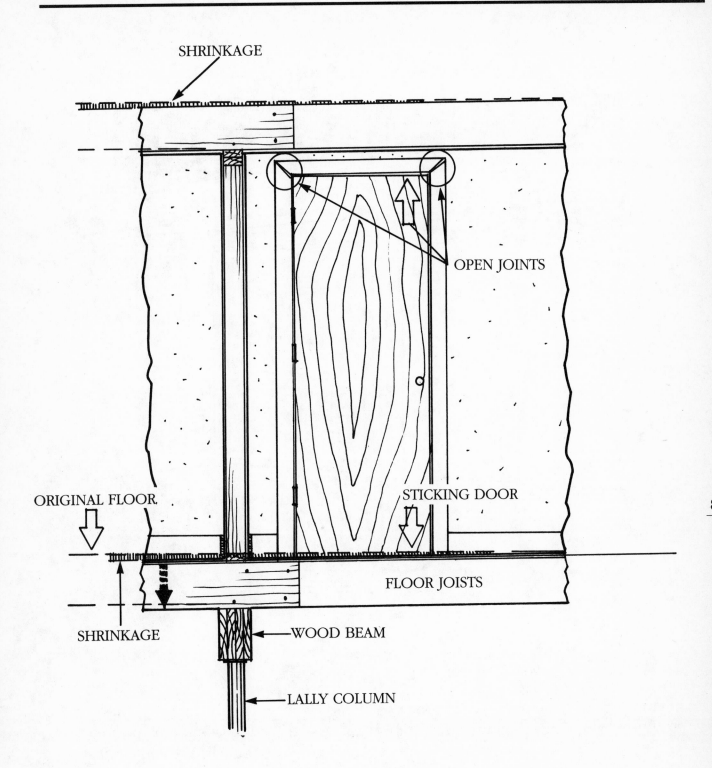

SHRINKAGE

OPEN JOINTS

ORIGINAL FLOOR

STICKING DOOR

87

FLOOR JOISTS

SHRINKAGE

WOOD BEAM

LALLY COLUMN

If you see gaps under baseboards, cracked walls (especially at the upper corner of door openings), gaps in trim joints, and doors that stick, go to the basement and you'll most likely find the dropped wood beam.

Main Carrying Beam

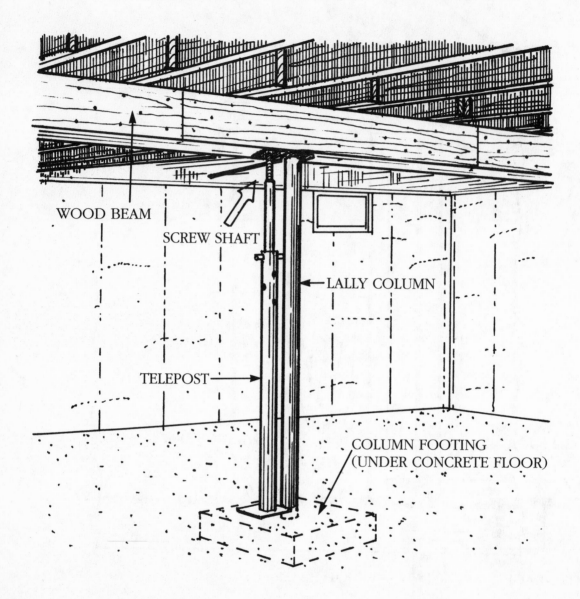

WOOD BEAM

SCREW SHAFT

LALLY COLUMN

TELEPOST

COLUMN FOOTING
(UNDER CONCRETE FLOOR)

Fortunately, all is not lost with the dropped wood-beam system. A "telepost" (tele-scoping post) or any post and jack combination can be used to jack up the beam. Just be sure to set your new posts or jacks close to the existing lally columns so that they'll bear on the column footings under the concrete floor.

The jacking has to be done a little at a time so as not to create new cracks in the walls. This can take weeks, depending on how bad things actually are. I recently inspected a house less than two years old that has a dropped wood beam and all the classic problems that follow. The beam has been in the process of being jacked up for two months, and it's not finished yet.

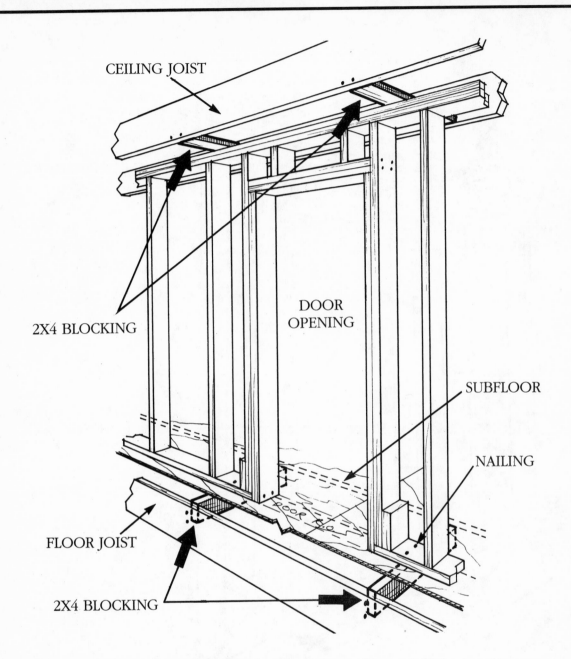

CEILING JOIST

2X4 BLOCKING

DOOR
OPENING

SUBFLOOR

NAILING

FLOOR JOIST

2X4 BLOCKING

At the bottom of both sides of door openings, there is a lot of nailing in many directions. The door frame is nailed in one direction, and the drywall, casings, and baseboards are nailed from both sides of the wall. If the door is going to hang properly in its frame, the bottom of each side of the opening has to be aligned accurately and anchored securely to the floor.

Blocks placed on edge between the floor joists on each side of the door opening stabilize this important area. You can check in the basement for this blocking.

Even where there isn't a door opening, there should be solid wood blocking every 24 inches under wall partitions that run parallel to the floor joists. Above, similarly spaced blocking should be laid flat between the ceiling joists. The result is solid nailing and adequate support for interior wall framing.

Interior Blocking

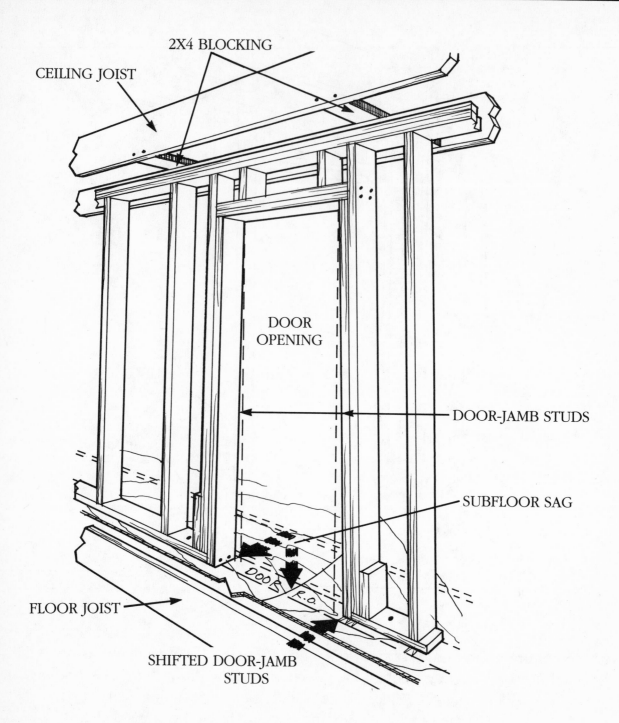

CEILING JOIST

2X4 BLOCKING

DOOR OPENING

DOOR-JAMB STUDS

SUBFLOOR SAG

FLOOR JOIST

SHIFTED DOOR-JAMB STUDS

This is what happens when there is no blocking under partitions that run parallel to the floor joists. The plywood subfloor isn't a good nailing surface, and it will sag under the weight of the partition. I have fixed these sags by jacking the floor up from the basement below and then nailing in the blocking that should have been put there when the house was built.

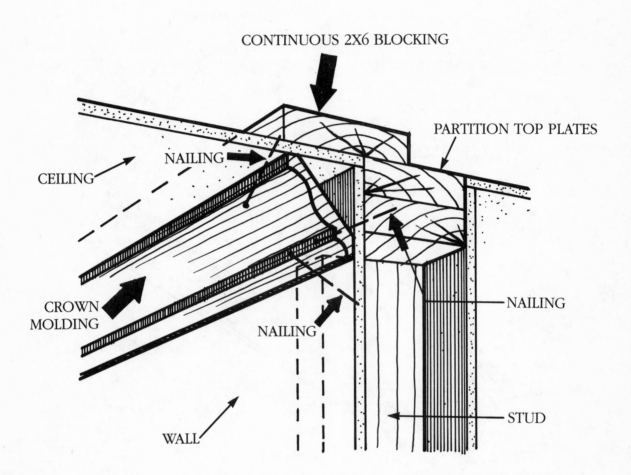

CONTINUOUS 2X6 BLOCKING

PARTITION TOP PLATES

NAILING

CEILING

CROWN
MOLDING

NAILING

NAILING

NAILING

STUD

WALL

Bad-looking trim work is often caused by inadequate blocking behind it to nail into. Large crown molding requires good nailing to pull it against ceiling and wall. A 2x4 or 2x6 nailed on the flat to the top partition plate provides nailing anywhere along the edge of the ceiling. The bottom edge of the molding is nailed into the studs.

Interior Blocking

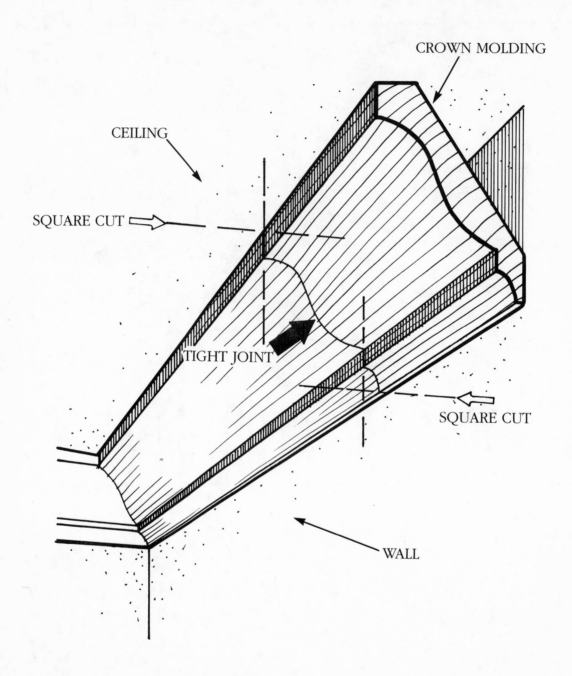

CROWN MOLDING

CEILING

SQUARE CUT

TIGHT JOINT

SQUARE CUT

WALL

Crown molding is easiest to install and looks best when mid-span joints are square cut. They can be cut a tad long and snapped in place, creating a pressure-tight joint that will always stay closed.

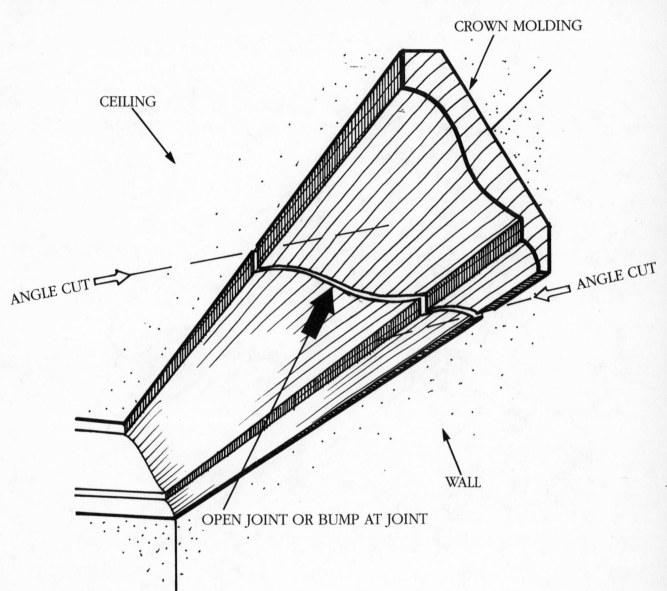

CEILING

CROWN MOLDING

ANGLE CUT

ANGLE CUT

WALL

OPEN JOINT OR BUMP AT JOINT

I've heard builders say (and I used to say) that the proper way to make a mid-span joint in interior trim is to angle-cut it. This doesn't work for two reasons: First, it's difficult to get a good fit with an angle cut. Second, the joint will change with the seasons: It will open up in the winter when the heat's on and bump up in the summer when the air is humid. (It has been said that wood does not shrink or expand along the grain. My experience with angle-cut trim tells me this isn't true.)

The best mid-span joint for trim work is the square-cut joint, cut just a tad long and snapped into place.

Interior Blocking

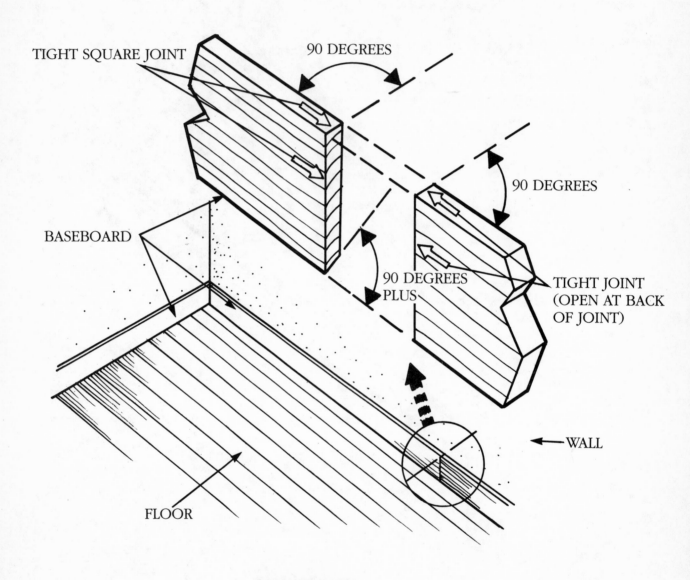

TIGHT SQUARE JOINT

90 DEGREES

90 DEGREES

BASEBOARD

90 DEGREES PLUS

TIGHT JOINT (OPEN AT BACK OF JOINT)

FLOOR

WALL

SQUARE CUT

Look for this mid-span joint in baseboards. When the sections are cut a tad long and snapped in place, the joint will stay tight forever. The cut is square down the front and across the top edge but relieved (back-cut) along the back edge so that only the visible front and top joints touch each other.

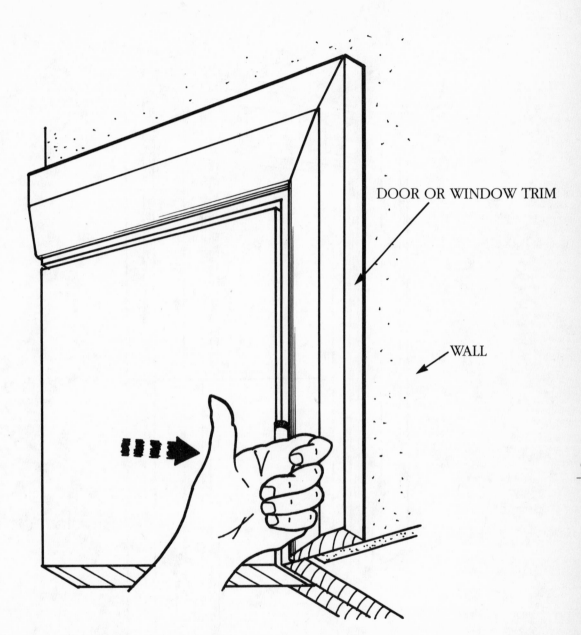

DOOR OR WINDOW TRIM

WALL

Check the trim nailing by rapping on the trim surface. A well-nailed piece of trim will sound solid. A not-so-well-nailed piece of trim will have a clacking sound, rapping once when your knuckle hits the trim and again when the loose trim hits the wall. Door and window casings are prime spots to check.

Interior Blocking

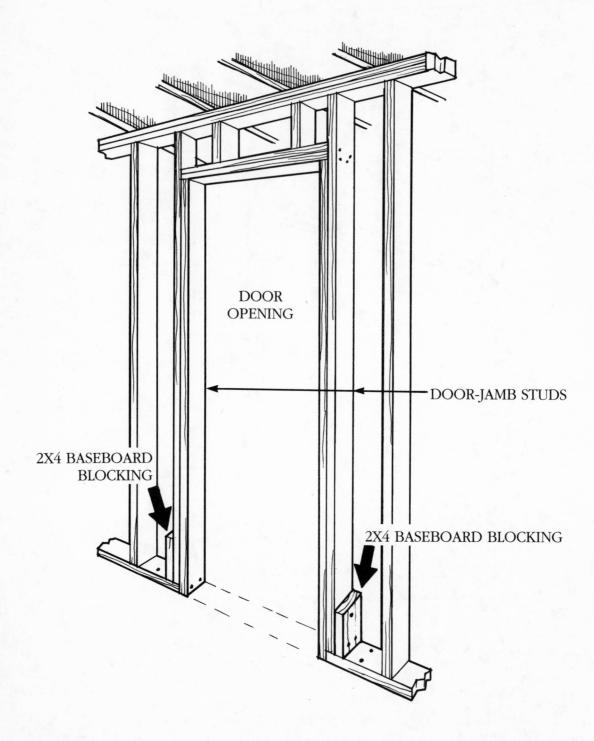

DOOR
OPENING

DOOR-JAMB STUDS

2X4 BASEBOARD
BLOCKING

2X4 BASEBOARD BLOCKING

When all the partitions are up, the natural next step is to put in all the trim blocking. Don't forget: For trim to be nailed securely, it needs solid wood behind it to nail into. Baseboards, for example, need a 2x4 block at the bottom of the door-jamb studs.

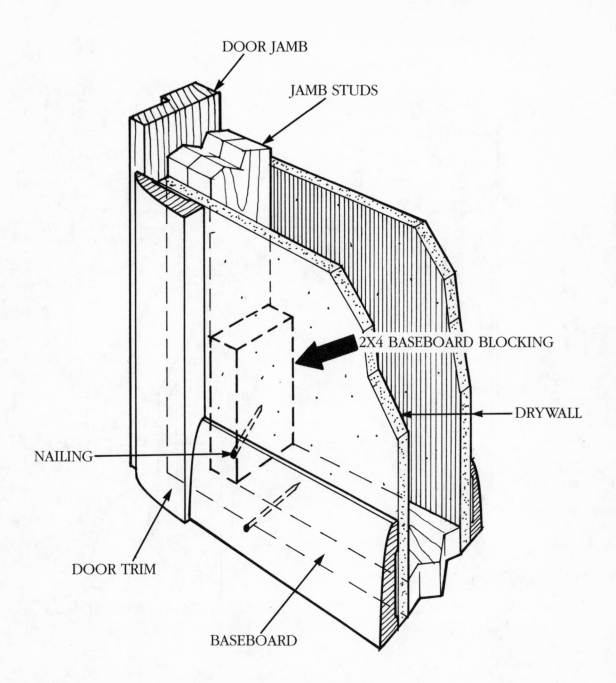

DOOR JAMB

JAMB STUDS

2X4 BASEBOARD BLOCKING

DRYWALL

NAILING

DOOR TRIM

BASEBOARD

This is how things look behind the wall at a door opening. The door trim usually covers most of the double jamb stud, so the added 2x4 block provides the necessary nailing at the end of the baseboard where it meets the door trim. Wider trim requires thicker blocking.

Interior Blocking

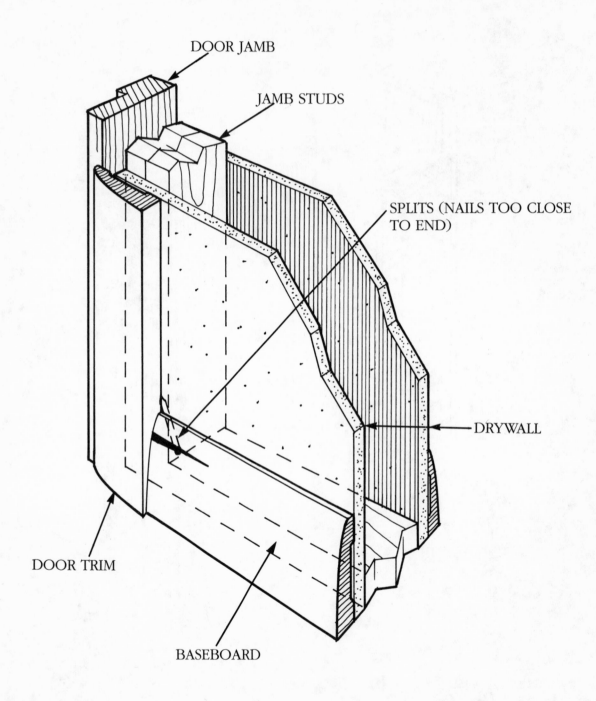

DOOR JAMB

JAMB STUDS

SPLITS (NAILS TOO CLOSE TO END)

DRYWALL

DOOR TRIM

BASEBOARD

When there is no blocking in the wall at a door opening, you're likely to find a split at the end of the baseboard. The carpenter made a nice fit at both ends of the baseboard, but without solid blocking back a few inches from the ends, it split when he nailed it into place. Rather than replace the baseboard (it would only split again), he patched the split. The patch might be difficult to detect at first, but it will become obvious as time passes.

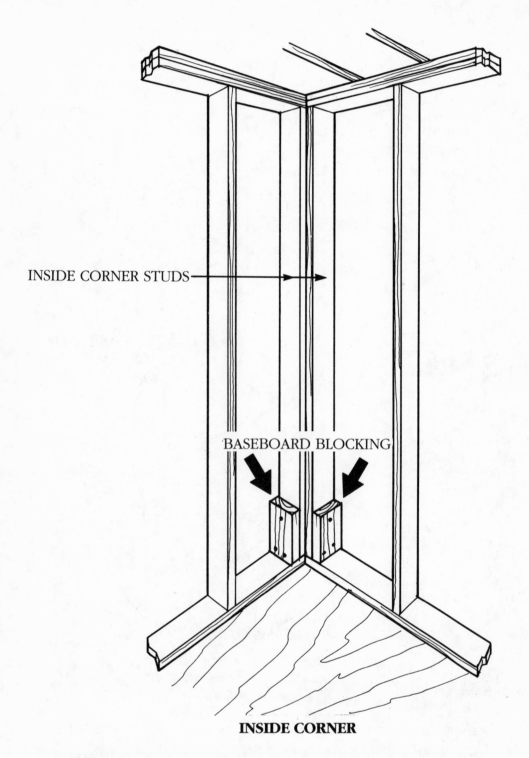

INSIDE CORNER STUDS

BASEBOARD BLOCKING

INSIDE CORNER

Inside corners need blocking, too. It's the same story: 2x4 blocks so that there's nail-ing at the top of the baseboard in the corner and far enough from the end so that the nail won't split the trim. It doesn't take much time to put the baseboard blocks in, and there are always enough scraps of wood around. They don't have to be cut to a specific length, just nailed in place.

Interior Blocking

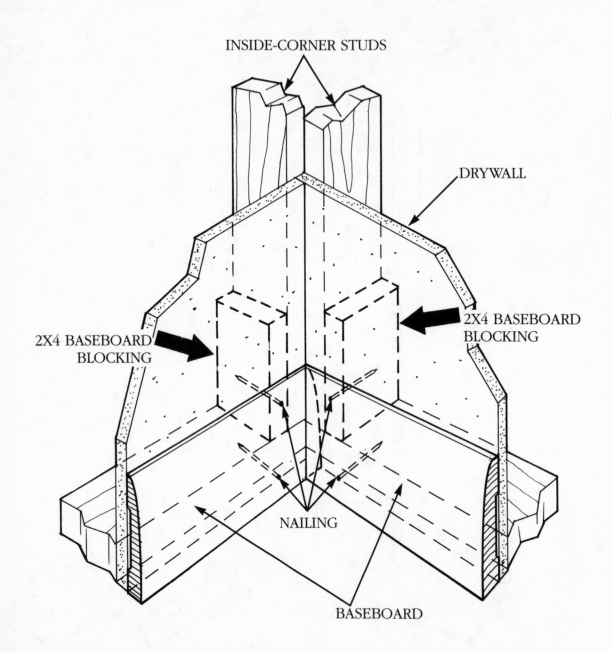

INSIDE-CORNER STUDS

DRYWALL

2X4 BASEBOARD
BLOCKING

2X4 BASEBOARD
BLOCKING

NAILING

BASEBOARD

This is what an inside corner should look like behind the walls. The inside-corner studs allow only 1 inch of nailing after the $1/2$-inch thickness for the drywall is taken into account. By adding 2x4 blocks, the solid nailing extends 2 $1/2$ inches from the corner in each direction.

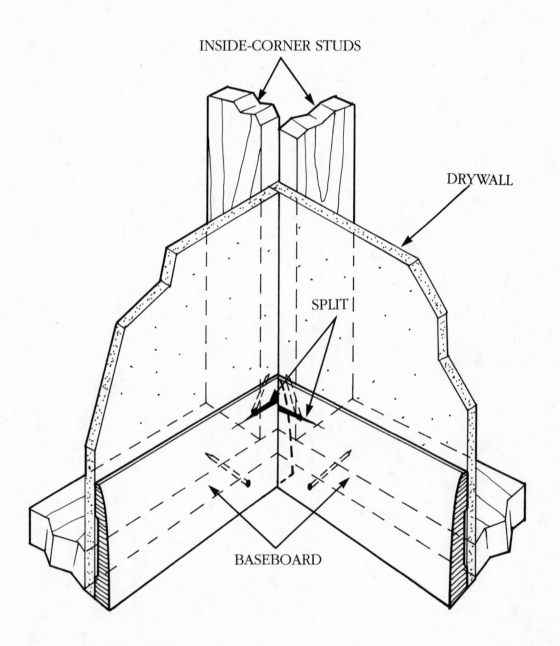

INSIDE-CORNER STUDS

DRYWALL

SPLIT

BASEBOARD

Take a look at the baseboards at inside corners. If there is no blocking behind the walls, you might find these patched splits. To avoid splitting when there's no blocking in place, a careful carpenter will predrill an angled nail hole. Anything that secures the baseboard in place is fine, but splits are *not* acceptable.

Interior Blocking

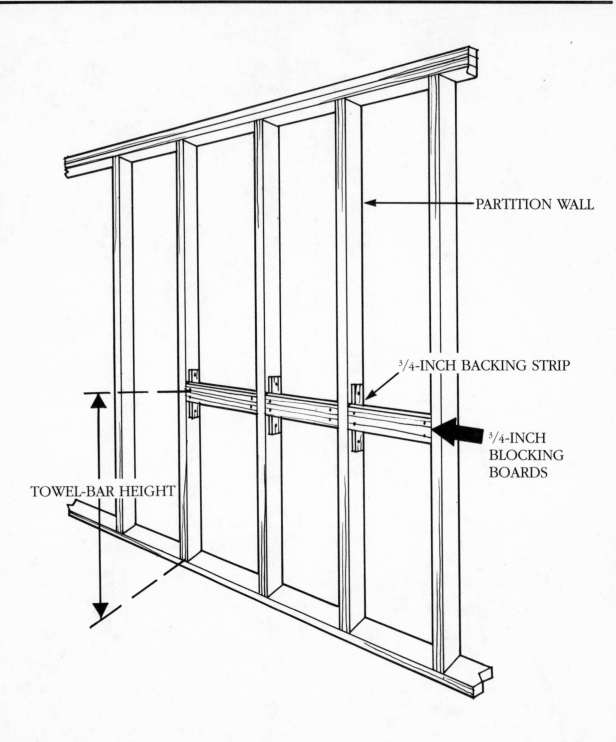

PARTITION WALL

¾-INCH BACKING STRIP

¾-INCH BLOCKING BOARDS

TOWEL-BAR HEIGHT

A good builder will provide plenty of blocking. A bathroom is a good example of the need for solid nailing surfaces behind the walls. Tub and shower stalls need blocking for nailing along their support flanges at the top and sides. Grab bars have to be well anchored. Even towel bars need light, ¾-inch blocking. The wider the blocking boards, the more leeway there is for height location.

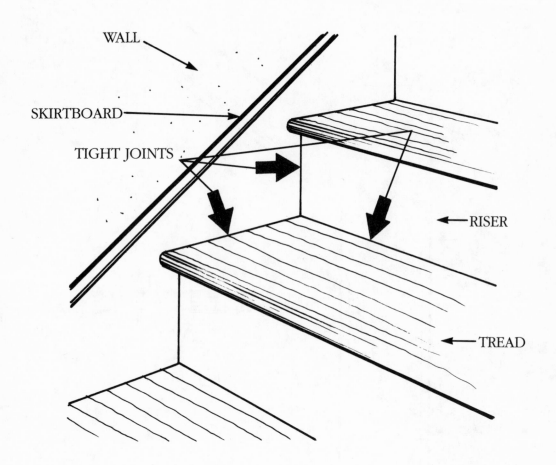

WALL

SKIRTBOARD

TIGHT JOINTS

RISER

TREAD

A well-built stairway should not squeak. Walk up and down the right side, left side, and middle of a stairway—you should hear nothing but your footfalls. Check for good tight joints where the risers and treads meet the skirtboard along the wall. Also check for good tight joints where the back of the treads meet the bottoms of the risers.

Stairs

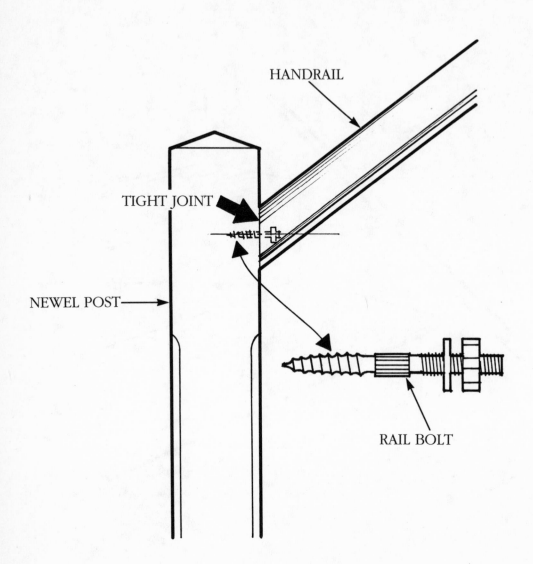

HANDRAIL

TIGHT JOINT

NEWEL POST

RAIL BOLT

Installing handrails on stairways is a difficult carpentry job. A place to check for good work is the joint where the handrail meets the newel post. You should find a good tight fit, securely fastened together with a rail bolt: a combination lag screw and nut and bolt. Nailing this joint together will not do.

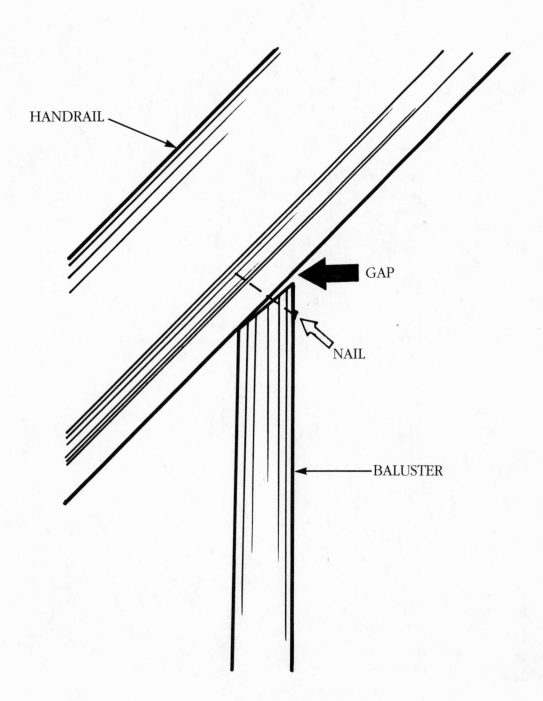

HANDRAIL

GAP

NAIL

BALUSTER

A carpenter's shortcut for installing balusters is to angle-cut the tops and toenail them to the bottom of the handrail. The resulting fit between the baluster and the rail is often bad. Worse, the baluster is sometimes split by the nailing. This is not a good way to install balusters.

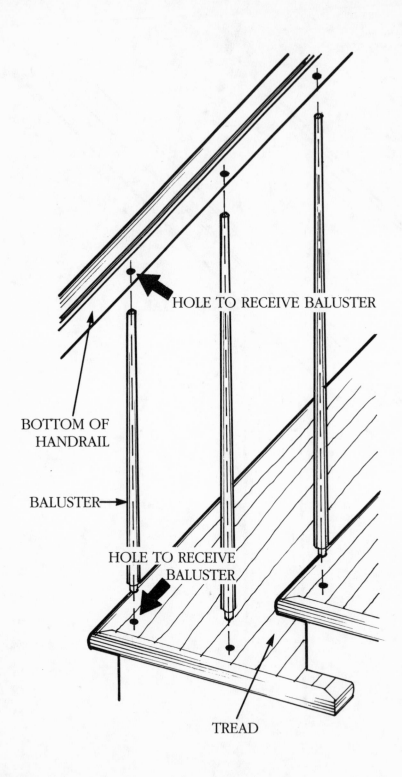

HOLE TO RECEIVE BALUSTER

BOTTOM OF
HANDRAIL

BALUSTER

HOLE TO RECEIVE
BALUSTER

TREAD

The best way to install balusters is to drill holes in the treads and in the bottom of the handrail to receive each baluster. It's a tough job, but a good stairbuilder wouldn't do it any other way.

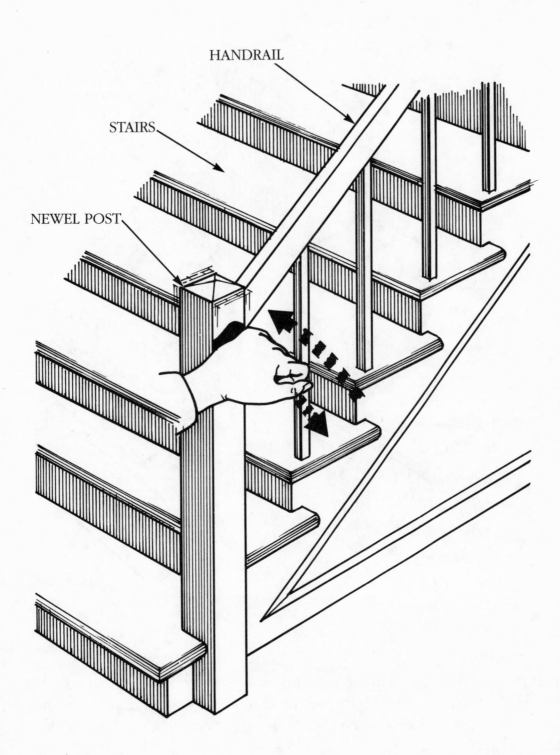

HANDRAIL

STAIRS

NEWEL POST

If you have a newel post, test how secure it is by punching the sides of the post with the side of your fist. It should feel and sound solid. A loose newel post only gets worse with use, and it isn't easy to fix one after the house is finished.

Stairs

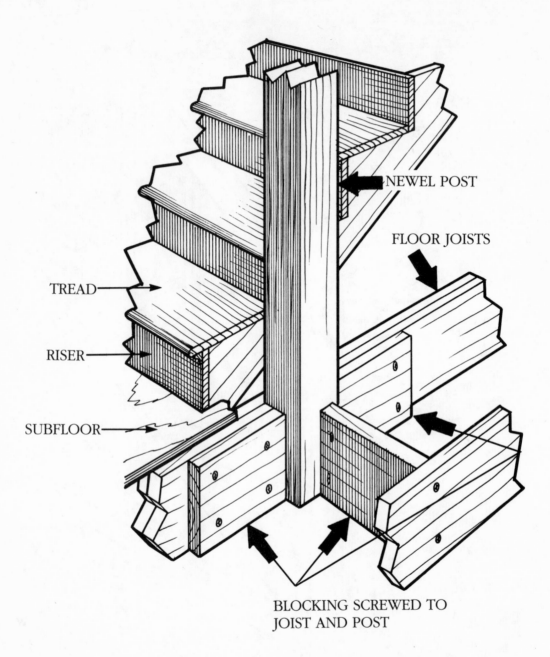

NEWEL POST

FLOOR JOISTS

TREAD

RISER

SUBFLOOR

BLOCKING SCREWED TO
JOIST AND POST

Check in the basement to see if the newel post is well anchored. It takes a lot of punishment and must be securely braced in all directions. Solid backing cut from floor joist material works best when it's wedged tightly against the sides of the work and screwed in place.

The blocking must be installed so that its ends, not its edges, brace the post. Major shrinkage occurs across the grain, and this, in time, would create a loose joint between blocks and post.

This newel-post anchoring system is just one of many ways that I've seen used, and it has worked well for me.

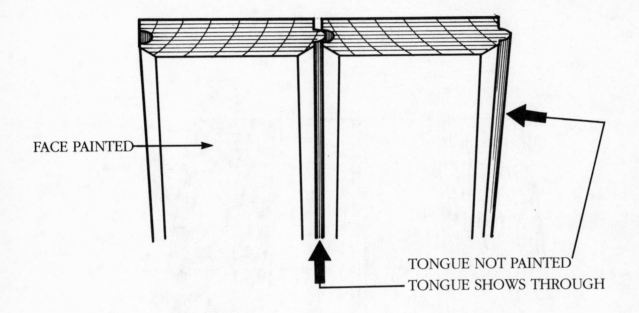

FACE PAINTED

TONGUE NOT PAINTED
TONGUE SHOWS THROUGH

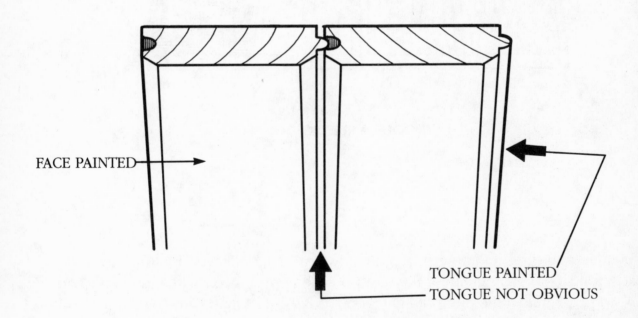

FACE PAINTED

TONGUE PAINTED
TONGUE NOT OBVIOUS

INTERIOR WOOD PANELING

A careful builder will paint or stain the tongues of interior wood paneling before installation. Even though interior tongue-and-groove paneling is nailed tight, the boards will shrink during dry time (usually winter, when the heat is turned on), revealing the tongue. Painting or staining the tongues will camouflage them so that the shrinkage cracks won't be so obvious.

Paneling

WILD GRAIN

PLAIN GRAIN

DARK WOOD

LIGHT WOOD

WOOD PANELING

A builder who cares about what he's doing when he installs wood paneling will match tone, color, and grain for the best possible appearance. Wild grain looks bad next to plain grain. One piece of light wood looks out of place on a dark wall, and vice-versa.

Not every builder has this sense. I was checking a job for a builder friend when I noticed that the paneling in the front entry had mostly medium-brown wood except for an oddball dark board here and there. Those boards really jumped out at me. My friend simply didn't understand what I was talking about.

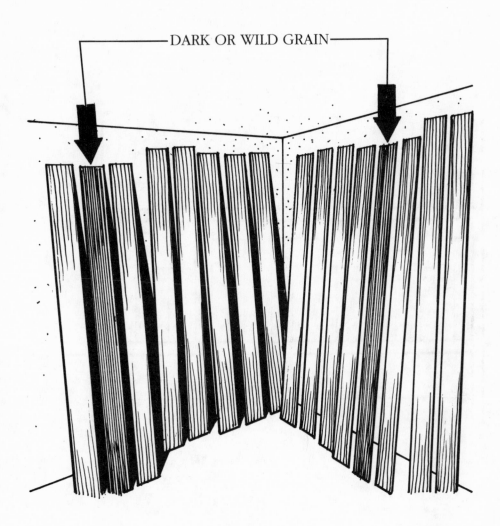

DARK OR WILD GRAIN

WOOD PANELING

You might want to match the panel boards yourself. A quick way to arrive at a good match is to arrange the boards around the room so you can easily spot the different surfaces. Then it's easy to put the most pleasing matches next to each other. The oddball panels can be cut for trim pieces.

Bookshelf Tip

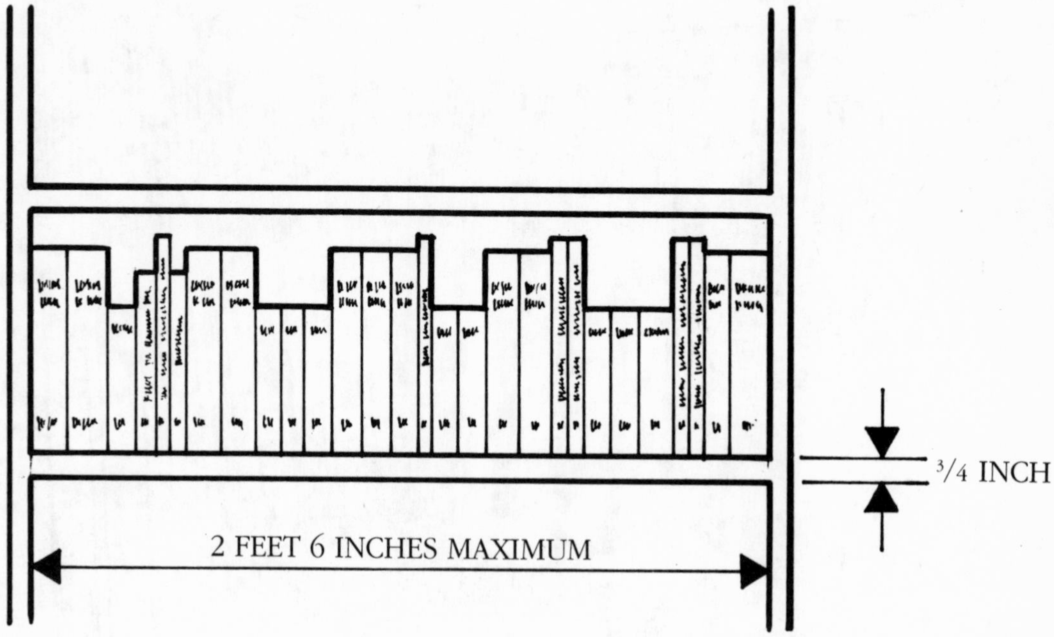

3/4 INCH

2 FEET 6 INCHES MAXIMUM

Nothing looks worse than sagging bookshelves. Pine shelves, 3/4 inch thick, should span no more than 2 feet, 6 inches. Thicker shelves or hardwood shelves can span more, but most bookshelves I have seen are 3/4-inch pine and usually sag.

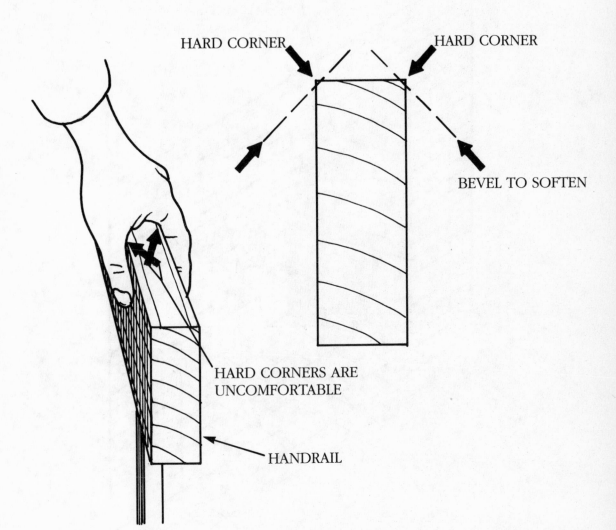

HARD CORNER   HARD CORNER

BEVEL TO SOFTEN

HARD CORNERS ARE
UNCOMFORTABLE

HANDRAIL

Square-cut trim as it comes from the lumberyard has hard corners along its edges. These edges dent easily, paint wears off, and they are uncomfortable to the touch. Check door frames, window frames, shelving, and handrails. The careful builder will soften these corners with a sharp block plane or sandpaper. Little details like these provide clues about quality, both seen and unseen, throughout the house.

Fireplace Cracks

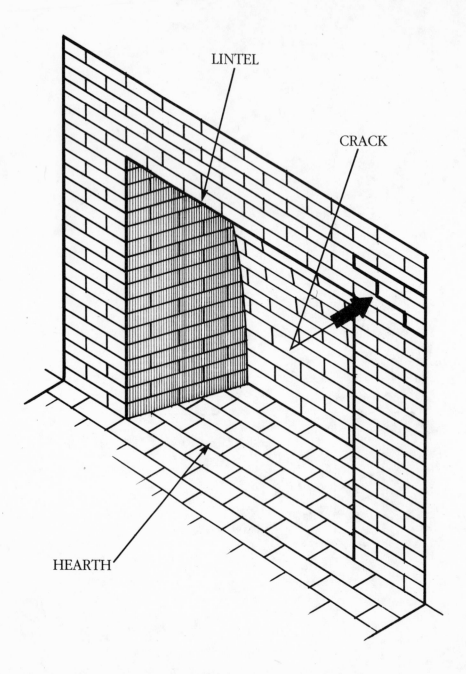

LINTEL

CRACK

HEARTH

It's all too common to find cracks on the fireplace wall. Structurally, this is no problem; the fireplace will not collapse. But it doesn't look too great. Most cracks in the fireplace wall are caused by the fire heating the angle-iron lintel over the opening. The lintel expands and pushes against the masonry, resulting in cracks at the weakest points. These cracks can never be repaired to look as good as new, because the joints are wider, and the old mortar color is almost impossible to match in the new mortar joints.

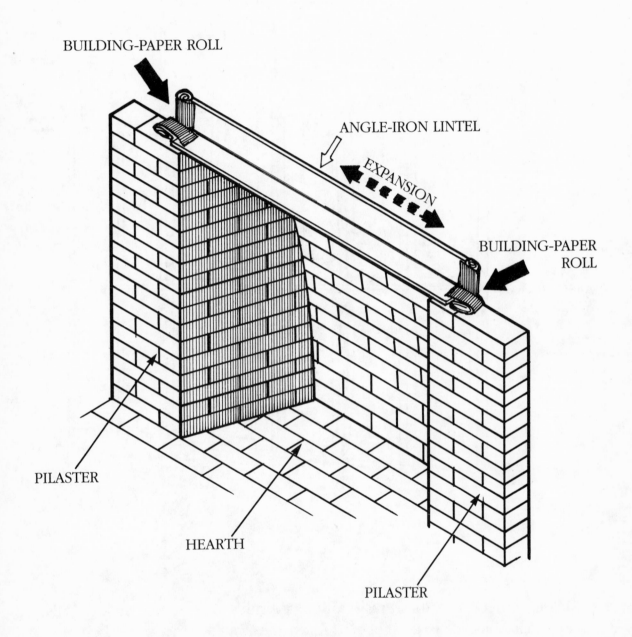

BUILDING-PAPER ROLL

ANGLE-IRON LINTEL

EXPANSION

BUILDING-PAPER ROLL

PILASTER

HEARTH

PILASTER

115

This is the system my mason uses to prevent fireplace cracks. His trick is keeping the masonry away from the ends of the angle-iron lintel. Rolled up strips of building paper (tar paper) at the ends of the lintel serve as expansion gaskets. The lintel can contract and expand freely. He takes the same precautions at the ends of the metal damper. If you're having your house built, make sure your mason is aware of this tip; but don't be surprised if he doesn't want to hear it.

Bowed Studs

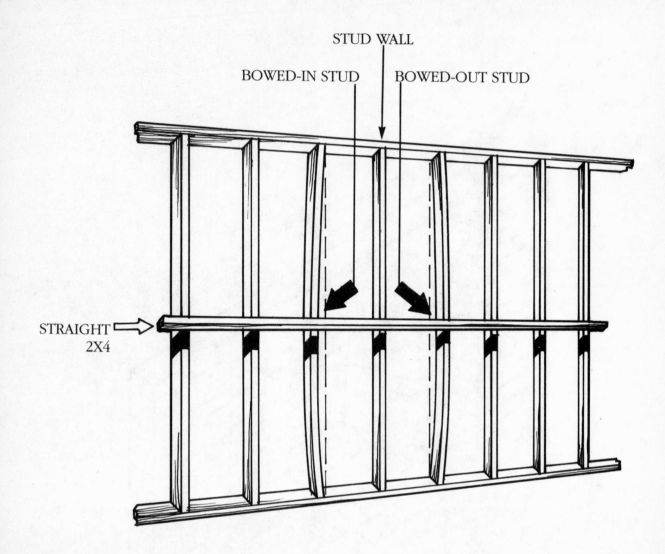

STUD WALL

BOWED-IN STUD   BOWED-OUT STUD

STRAIGHT
2X4

If you're building, check the cabinet walls for bowed studs, using a straight 2x4. This used to be standard practice years ago, but I know most builders no longer bother. Holding a long straight 2x4 against the studs of an interior partition (exterior partitions are usually straightened by the exterior sheathing) will reveal the bowed stud.

When two studs are bowed in opposite directions, one toward you and the other away, the stud bowed away might not show up until the other is straightened. It's often easier to replace a badly bowed stud than to straighten it, but at this stage of the job, studs often seem to be scarce.

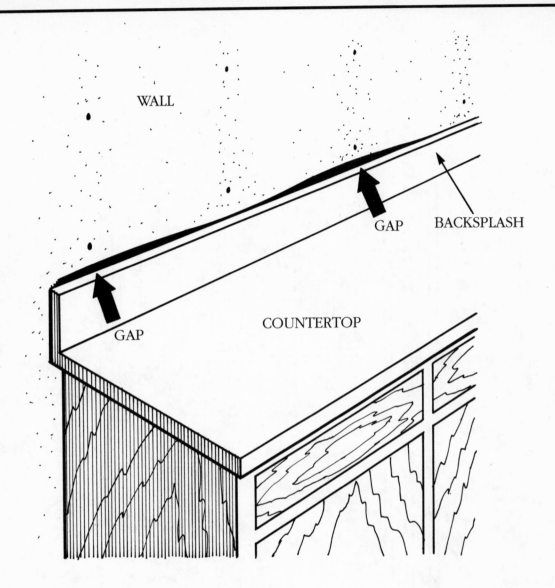

WALL

GAP   BACKSPLASH

GAP

COUNTERTOP

Check the backsplash on countertops to see if the walls have been straightened. It is very difficult to hang cabinets and fit countertops well on walls that are not straight. Counters should always be scribe-fit to the wall. Bowed studs make this already time-consuming job a lot tougher.

To scribe-fit the counter backsplash, position it against the wall. You'll notice that there are gaps. Set a small compass—the kind you used in school to make circles—to the size of the largest gap. Then run the metal point of the compass against the wall and the pencil of the compass along the top of the backsplash. The resulting wavy pencil line will mimic any ripples in the wall. Trimming the backsplash to this line should result in a perfect fit. (A straight, flat wall needs very little cut off.)

Cabinets hung on a bowed-out stud will be out of plumb unless they too are scribed to hang plumb. On a badly bowed wall, you sometimes can't scribe enough to compensate. It's quicker, and neater in the end, to straighten the bowed studs before the drywall is installed.

Bowed Studs

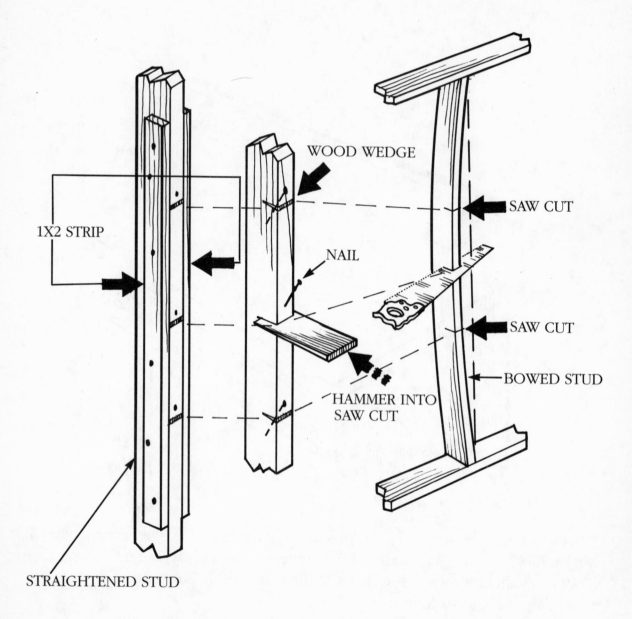

WOOD WEDGE

SAW CUT

1X2 STRIP

NAIL

SAW CUT

BOWED STUD

HAMMER INTO
SAW CUT

STRAIGHTENED STUD

118

It's easy to straighten bowed studs. It requires cutting with a handsaw, a little shimming with wood-shingle tips, then splinting up the stud with wood strips nailed on
each side. If you see that this has been done in a house being built for you, you
have a careful builder.

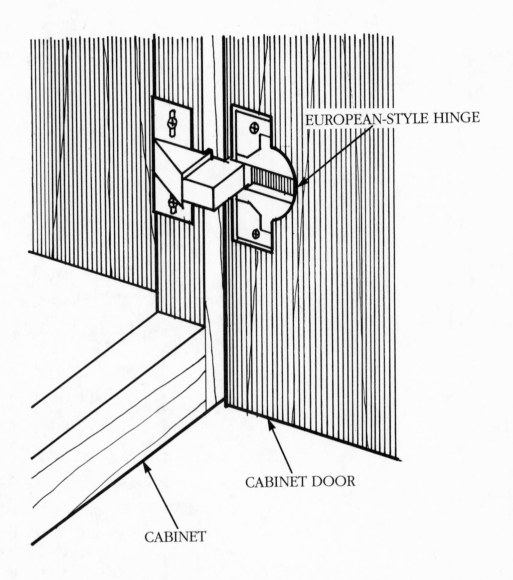

EUROPEAN-STYLE HINGE

CABINET DOOR

CABINET

Most people can't tell the difference between a well-built cabinet and one that's not so well built. The reason is that these days there's not that much difference in construction or materials. (The exception is the custom-built cabinet.) One detail some manufacturers cut corners with is the hardware. Doors should open and shut smoothly. Look for European-style hinges. They adjust easily, work smoothly and are self-closing. Drawers should open and close smoothly, too, with no side-to-side movement. Look for ball-bearing slides on each side of the drawers. The cheapest slides have nylon rollers.

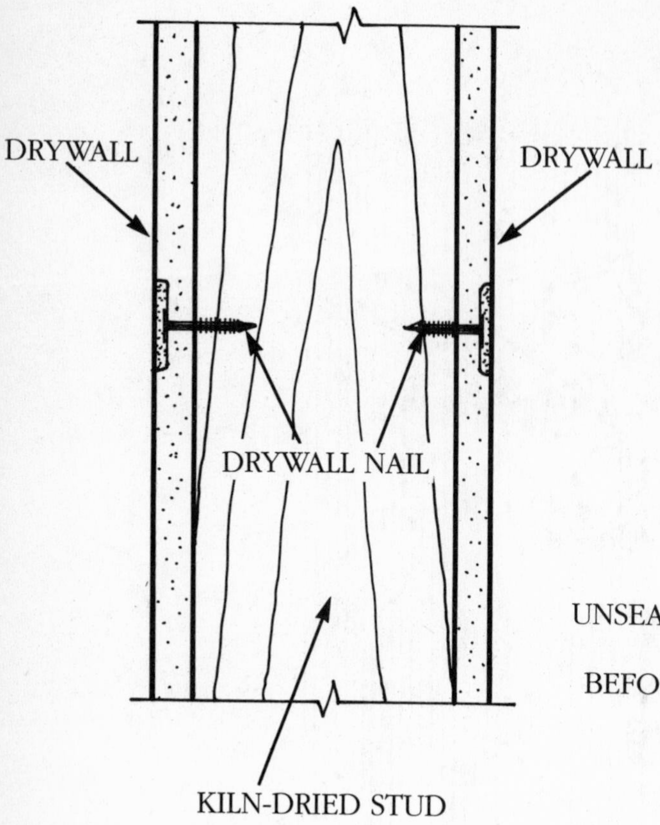

Drywall

DRYWALL

DRYWALL

DRYWALL NAIL

KILN-DRIED STUD

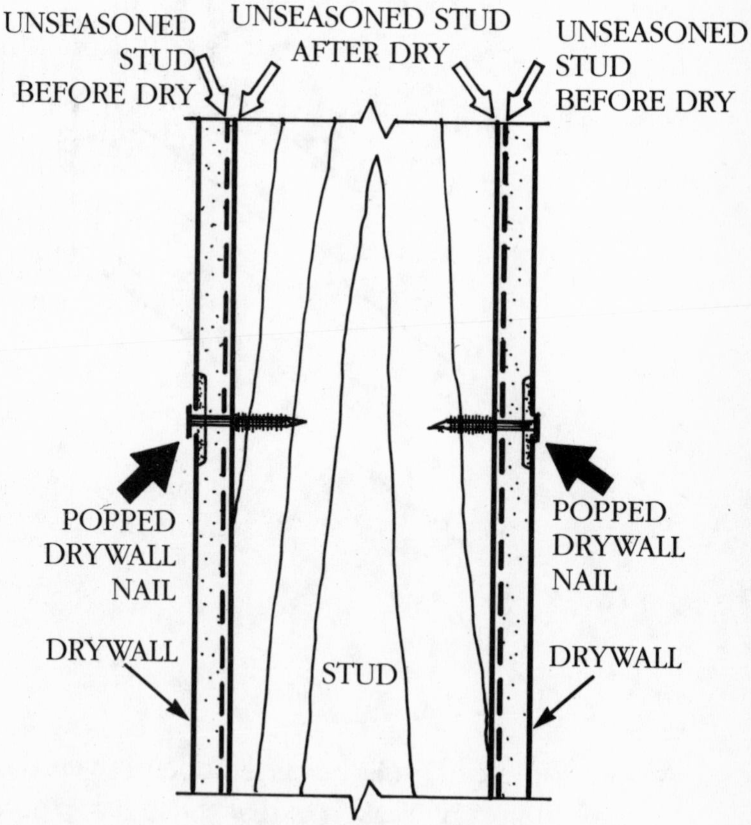

120

UNSEASONED STUD BEFORE DRY

UNSEASONED STUD AFTER DRY

UNSEASONED STUD BEFORE DRY

POPPED DRYWALL NAIL

POPPED DRYWALL NAIL

DRYWALL

STUD

DRYWALL

"Nail popping" occurs when unseasoned lumber is used in drywall construction. Here, kiln-dried framing lumber is a must. If unseasoned framing lumber is used, make sure the framed house is dried out by using heaters. All good builders do this.

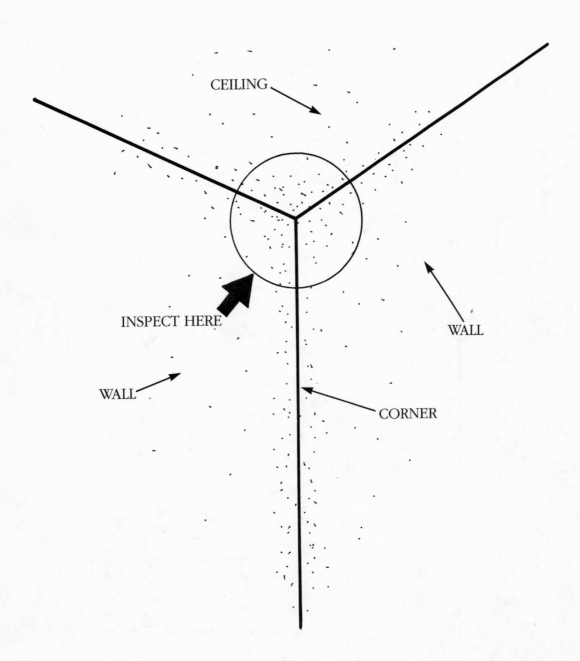

A good drywall job must have neat, crisp corners. The first place to inspect is where the ceiling meets two intersecting walls.

Drywall

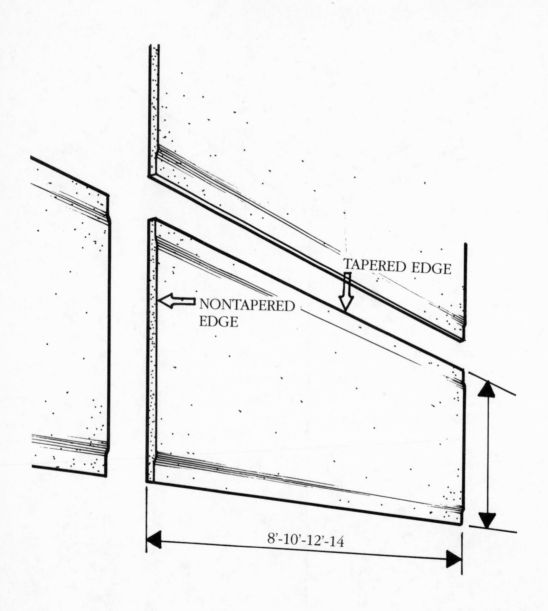

TAPERED EDGE

NONTAPERED EDGE

8'-10'-12'-14

All drywall sheets have two tapered edges and two nontapered edges. It's always preferable to put the tapered edges together for a good, unobtrusive finished seam called, naturally enough, a tapered seam. Unfortunately the nontapered edges have to be butted to each other, too. This results in a butt seam, and achieving a finished look with this seam is much more difficult.

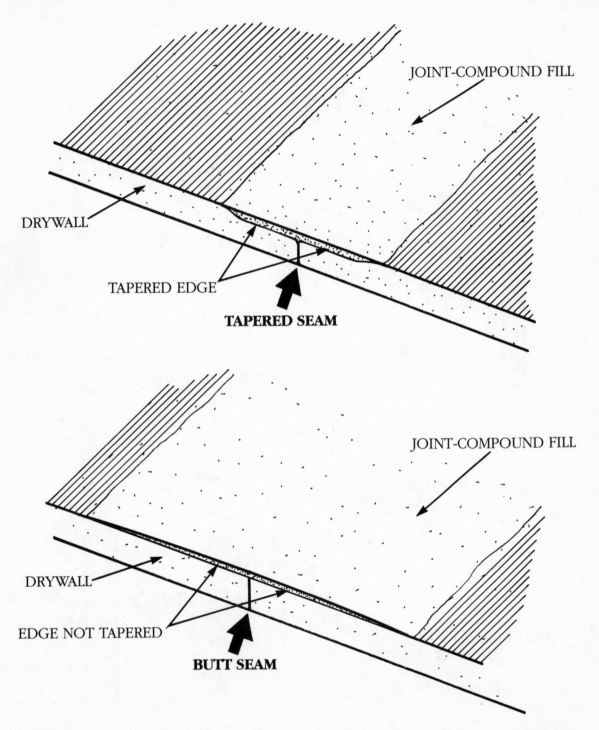

JOINT-COMPOUND FILL

DRYWALL

TAPERED EDGE

TAPERED SEAM

JOINT-COMPOUND FILL

DRYWALL

EDGE NOT TAPERED

BUTT SEAM

Taping is the key to unobtrusive seams. Make sure tapered seams are filled flush. Make sure butt seams are feathered far enough out so they don't show a bulge when a light is shined along the wall or ceiling.

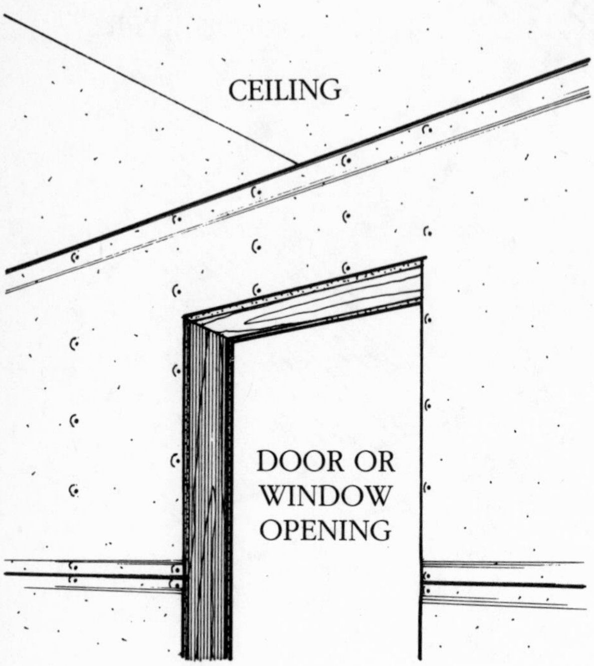

Drywall

CEILING

**ONE PIECE OF DRYWALL
CUT OUT FOR OPENING**

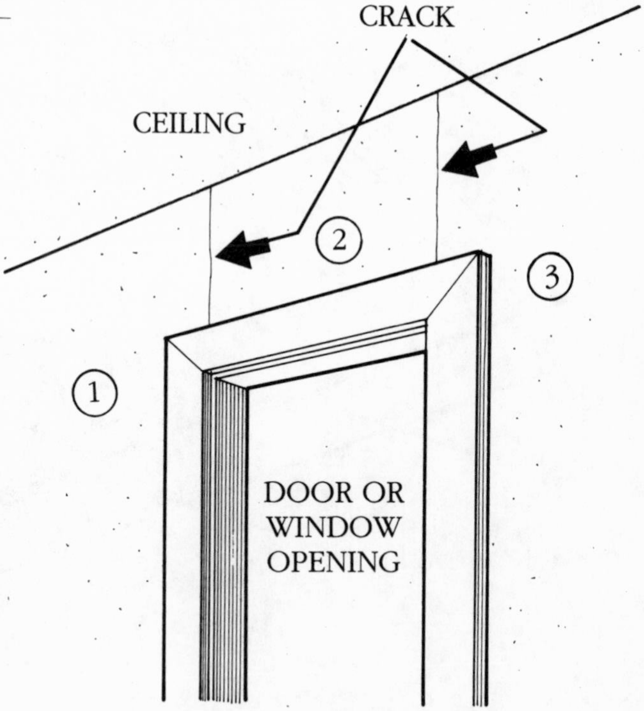

DOOR OR
WINDOW
OPENING

CRACK

CEILING

②

①

③

DOOR OR
WINDOW
OPENING

**THREE PIECES OF DRYWALL
AT OPENING**

These cracks often occur over window and door openings when drywall is installed in three pieces in these areas. It's more difficult to install a single piece, but I always do it when I hang the drywall myself, and I ask for this when someone else is hanging the drywall. I usually get what I want, so the openings are usually done right.

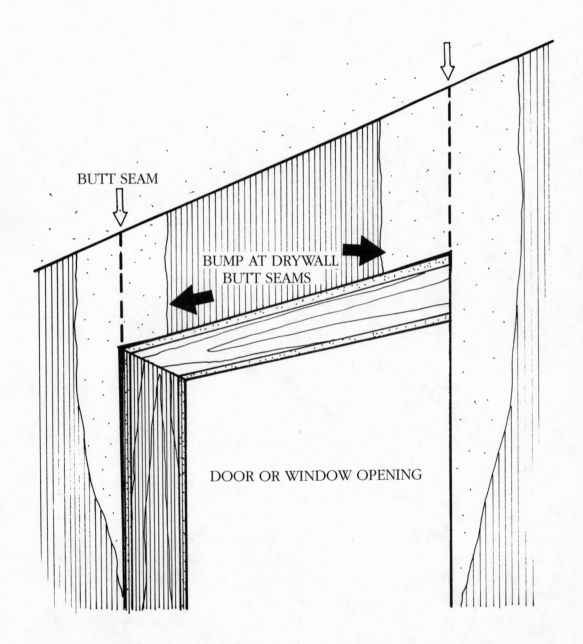

BUTT SEAM

BUMP AT DRYWALL
BUTT SEAMS

DOOR OR WINDOW OPENING

Another reason for avoiding the joints at the corners of window and door openings is that the bump created at these joints by even well-feathered taping compound makes it difficult to make good trim joints in these areas. A careful carpenter will compensate for these irregularities and make good trim joints and tight fits against the wall.

Flooring

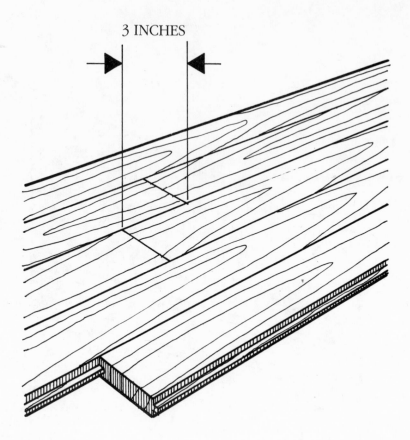

3 INCHES

A good builder will take the following precautions before laying hardwood strip flooring:

First, three weeks before the flooring is delivered, the thermostat is set to 70 degrees or so. This is to dry out the house. And second, the flooring is delivered at least three days before it is to be installed. Each bundle of flooring is opened, allowing the wood to adjust to the moisture in the house.

Butt joints must be staggered a minimum of 3 inches. Nailing (or stapling) should be into every joist, with one nail between joists. So when you look at the underside of the subfloor from the basement, you should see one row of nails or staples between each row of floor joists.

I recently examined a house for faulty construction, and one of the problems was an incorrectly installed oak strip floor. The flooring ran in the direction of the short dimension of the room. It squeaked badly, and there were many cracks between the oak boards. The builder, not knowing how to install flooring, used a nailgun with shingle staples, and once in a while, he stapled into a joist. The subfloor underneath looked like a porcupine.

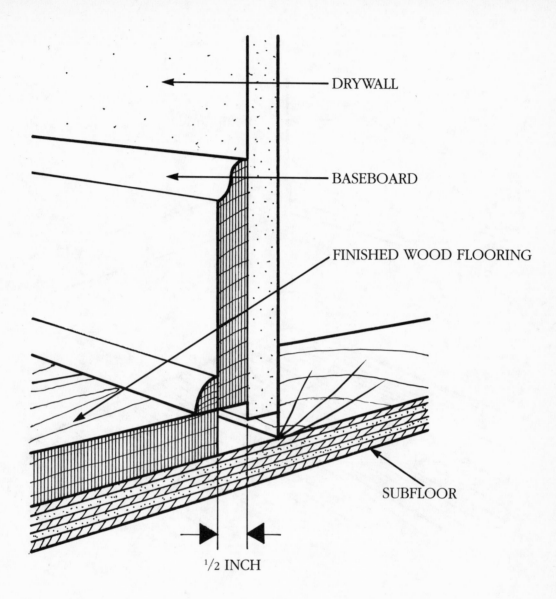

DRYWALL

BASEBOARD

FINISHED WOOD FLOORING

SUBFLOOR

¹/₂ INCH

It's usually best to run strip flooring in the direction of the room's longest dimension. Because wood expands and contracts across the grain (the rule of thumb here is ¹/₁₆-inch expansion and contraction per foot of flooring boards), there will be less movement across the short dimension of the room. A 16-foot by 32-foot room would have a potential expansion of 1 inch across the 16-foot dimension and 2 inches across the 32-foot dimension.

A good floor installer will leave a minimum gap of ¹/₂ inch between flooring and wall. I have seen floors buckle and walls shift because no gap was left between the flooring and the wall.

If the flooring runs parallel to the floor joists, make sure an additional layer of ⁵/₈-inch plywood (not particleboard; it doesn't hold nails well) is glued and nailed over the subfloor.

Flooring

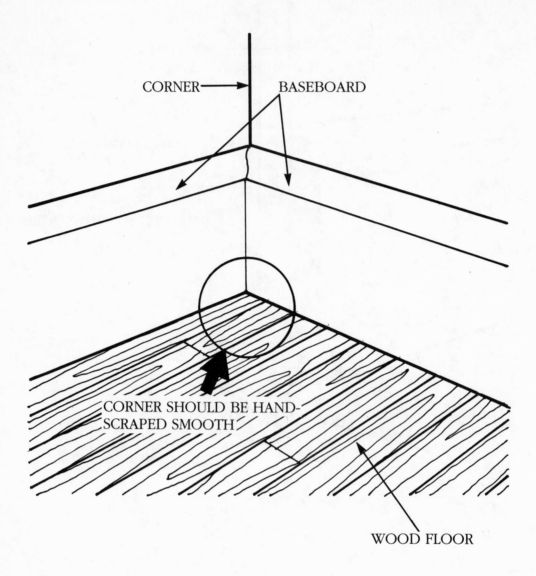

CORNER → BASEBOARD

CORNER SHOULD BE HAND-SCRAPED SMOOTH

WOOD FLOOR

New floors that aren't "prefinished" have to be sanded. I have used many floor-sanding professionals, and it's tough to find a good one. The place to check for good work is in the corners. The good professional will scrape the corners smooth with a razor-sharp paint scraper.

There are two types of floor finishes: surface finishes and penetrating finishes. A surface finish, like urethane or varnish, leaves a tough skin on top of the wood. Penetrating finishes are absorbed by the wood until many coats create a buildup on the surface. The best finish I know of is called a Swedish finish, which combines the qualities of the surface finish and the penetrating finish.

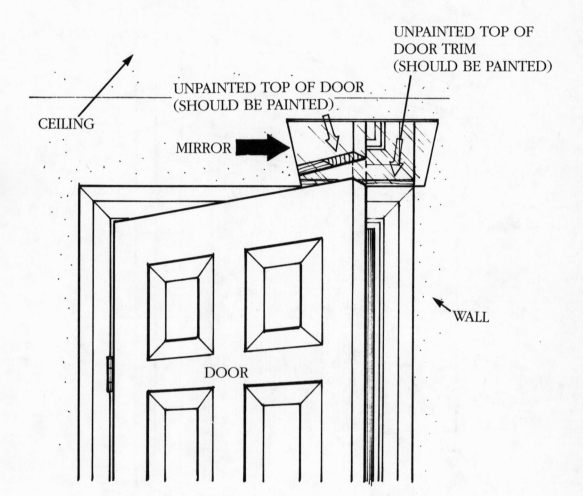

CEILING

UNPAINTED TOP OF DOOR
(SHOULD BE PAINTED)

UNPAINTED TOP OF
DOOR TRIM
(SHOULD BE PAINTED)

MIRROR

WALL

DOOR

129

Check the tops and bottoms of doors to make sure they are painted. If they're stained instead, make sure they're sealed, too, just like the surface of the doors. Staining raises the grain and actually invites more water into the wood. These days urethane is the standard sealant. Skipping door tops and bottoms is a common shortcut. A mirror will tell the story. Take special care to be sure that any end-grain is carefully sealed.

Door Tips

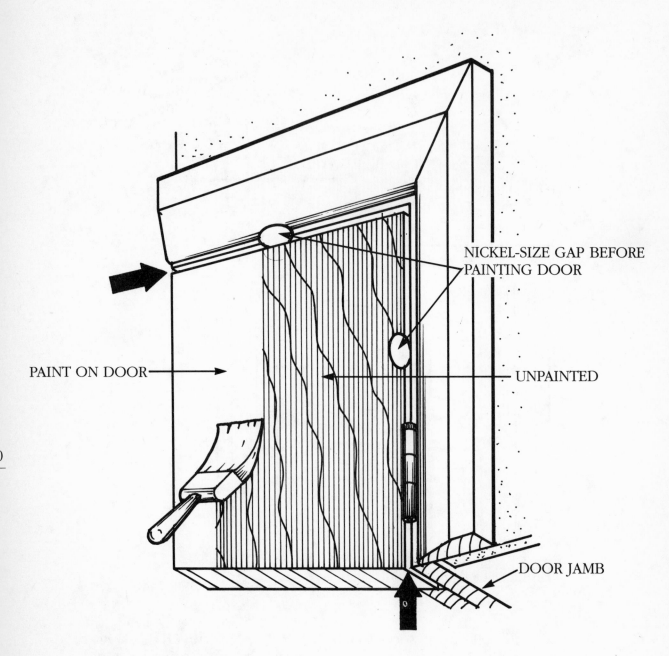

NICKEL-SIZE GAP BEFORE PAINTING DOOR

PAINT ON DOOR

UNPAINTED

DOOR JAMB

Check the gaps between door and door frame. Proper gaps at the door edges are important to keep the door from sticking. A painted door should have a gap just the thickness of a nickel before painting.

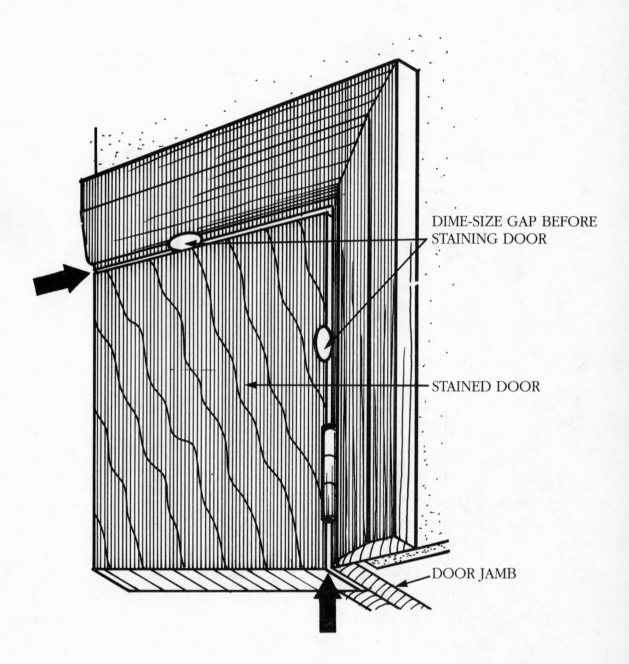

DIME-SIZE GAP BEFORE STAINING DOOR

STAINED DOOR

DOOR JAMB

131

The proper gap for stained doors is the thickness of a dime before staining and sealing. (Remember, tops and bottoms should also be stained and sealed.)

Door Tips

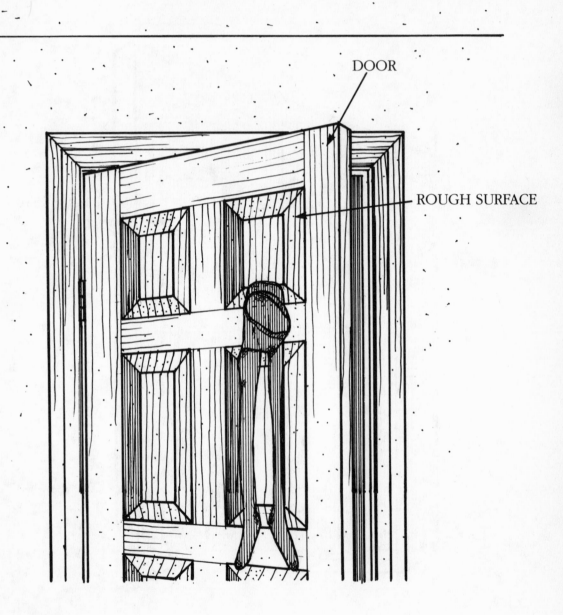

DOOR

ROUGH SURFACE

Another common shortcut is to skimp on the use of sandpaper. Sanding takes time, but it's the difference between a good paint job and a poor paint job. Each coat of paint, stain, and sealer must be sanded and dusted before the next coat is applied. When this sanding process is omitted, the surface feels rough to the touch. The roughness can be bad enough to snag (or even hang) pantyhose. The last coat, however, should not be sanded.

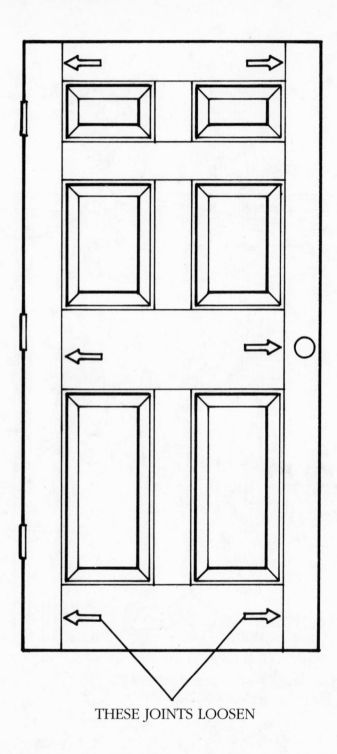

THESE JOINTS LOOSEN

Naturally, entry doors should operate smoothly. The joints of a sticky or binding door will eventually loosen, which will worsen the condition and even ruin the door. Steel doors are a good choice here, but they're not as good-looking as wood doors.

Door Tips

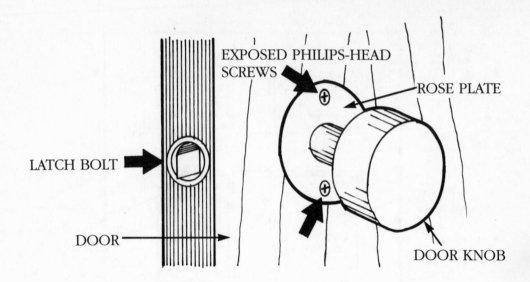

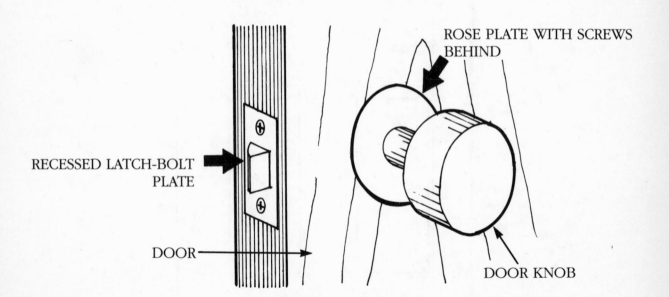

Check the hardware on interior doors. They should all have three hinges. Two hinges will work for a while, but three will keep a door hanging straight and swinging smoothly for years.

Check the lockset, too. Cheap locksets have their latch bolt housed in a simple cylinder. Their attachment screws are exposed, too. These locksets don't hold up well. The screws require frequent tightening, and the latch-bolt cylinder sometimes loosens.

Better locksets have latch-bolt front plates that are recessed and screwed into the edge of the door. Their screw-fastening systems are superior, and the screws are covered by an outside rose plate. The best locksets cost. Most companies offer different qualities. Don't go by brand name alone. You get what you pay for.

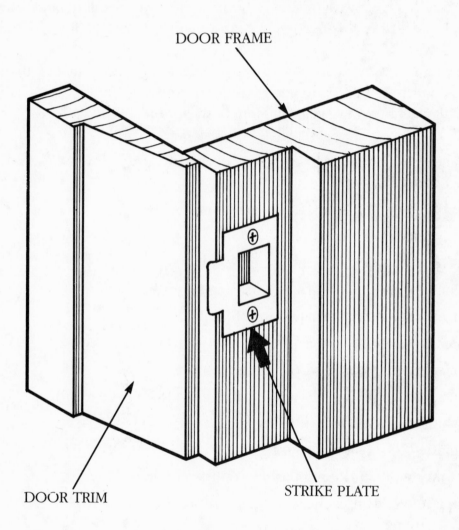

DOOR FRAME

DOOR TRIM

STRIKE PLATE

135

Check the latch-bolt front plate and the strike plate. A good craftsman will install them so they look as if they were cast in place.

Review with a "Roving Eye"

I always have a roving eye whenever I visit a house, new or old. I can tell pretty quickly if the builder knows his craft. So whenever I am called on to examine a house, I use the same technique—the roving eye.

I start by standing well away from the house to get an overall general impression. Most look great from this perspective, and many a house is purchased as a result of this view.

Then I move in close to check the quality of the work—first outside, then inside. This is where you can tell if you're getting a good house.

You can cultivate a roving eye, too. Here is what you should look for.

1. Ground should slope away from house, especially at window wells and ground-level doors.

2. Level entry steps with neat masonry work; no cracks.

3. Wood trim spaced off masonry.

4. Well-put-together wood trim; no splits or warps.

5. Neat siding job; no splits, warps, or missing shingles.

6. Three-coat paint job with nails set and filled.

7. Neat gutter installation, with proper slope toward downspouts.

8. Proper offset of joints on a wood-shingle roof.

9. A straight roof-shingle line along the gable ends from eave to ridge.

10. Straight shingle line along roof valleys.

11. A good grade of asphalt shingles.

12. Neat masonry work and good flashing on the chimney.

13. Neat concrete work on garage floor and apron; no cracks. A plus is a dropped apron with an angle iron at the drop.

14. A smoothly operating front door; no binding.

15. Floor free of squeaks and laid up tight, with proper joint stagger.

16. Baseboard trim hard against the floor; no gaps.

17. Good baseboard joints at corners and doors, well nailed with no splits.

18. Good joints in door and window trim, well nailed with a smooth finish.

19. Easily operating windows with no sticking.

20. Well-fitted doors showing an equal space all around between door and frames.

21. Three hinges on all doors and a good grade of hardware.

22. Neat installation of door hardware.

23. Smooth finish on all doors, stained or painted, with tops and bottoms painted or stained and sealed.

24. Neat drywall joints, no nail pops, and crack-free over doors and windows.

25. Book shelves ³/₄ inch thick spanning no more than 2 feet, 6 inches.

26. Neat joints at countertops with a good fit against the wall.

27. Good grade of cabinet hardware.

28. Neat, clean fireplace masonry work. Narrow mortar joints in brickwork look best.

29. Solid newel posts at stairways. Good joint where handrail meets newel post.

30. Nonsqueaking stairs.

31. Balusters set into handrail and tread, not toenailed.

32. Good joint where tread meets the wall trim (stringer).

33. Dry basement; no water stains on walls or floor.

34. Crack-free walls. Snap-tie holes filled.

35. Minimum number of floor cracks. They are almost impossible to avoid; one or two acceptable.

36. The main beam in the basement should be steel. If the main beam is wood, it must be of the flush type, not a dropped beam.